Diary of a Platonic Co-Parent

Nick Farrow

Published by Nick Farrow, 2024.

Introduction

My name is Nick. I am 54 years old and I am a fortunate man. I have the most beautiful 8-year-old daughter called Milly and a wonderful friendship with her mother Rae. Rae and I are platonic co-parents, and this is my diary of our journey. It is a warts and all story of how I came to be in this relationship and the difficulties and decisions I've had to make along the way. This is not a guide to co-parenting. I am not endorsing or advising you to copy any of the methods and techniques we have used. There is no universally correct method for co-parenting. We did it our way. I address the issues that came up for us and how we, as intentional co-parents, navigated them. It could serve as an insight for anyone who is interested in this alternative family setup or who is maybe thinking of embarking on it themselves. I raise issues along the way and I invite you to reflect on how they may relate to your particular circumstances. This story begins in 2011, when I was 42, in a city on the south coast of England called Brighton. A place that is so incredibly liberal and diverse; it seems like there is a rainbow family on every corner. It was the perfect platform from which to launch our family adventure.

Before we get started, however, I feel I should share a bit about myself. This is never easy, but here goes. Some of my more positive personality traits are creativity, playfulness, a strong work ethic, and a spirit of never giving up. Trying to be kind to people is important to me and I am thankful I make friends easily. Alongside this, I can also be overly sensitive, self-doubting, and even paranoid. I somehow hold a delicate balance of adventurous and anxious tendencies. This combination means that although I don't always find life easy, it is rarely boring. I am an incurable liberal with a sense of spirituality that makes Mystic Meg look like Richard Dawkins. (Don't worry, I don't bark on about it in this book). I spent much of my twenties as the singer in various post-punk bands, trying desperately to become the world's next Robert

Smith. Amongst the flashing lights, drugs and makeup, it didn't dawn on me once that I would actually need talent to achieve such an ambition. In my mind, part of me is still that ambitious young goth, unfortunately I look more like Homer Simpson these days. Life doesn't always turn out the way you want it. My values are most closely aligned with that of a humanist. For me, no culture, religion or belief system holds the monopoly on truth. I am eclectic and judge actions on how much they spread happiness. Since a very young age, I have felt that people are, at their core, good (in most cases).

During my networking with other co-parents, when I was first learning about it, I was lucky to meet quite a few same-sex co-parents to get advice from. It seemed, however, that Rae and I were the only heterosexual people locally taking this alternative family path. It felt as if we were sailing into unchartered waters. When I was researching for this book, I went onto a parenting forum and asked, 'If I told you, I was going to become a platonic co-parent. (Which is a conscious decision to have a child with someone that you're not in a romantic relationship with). What questions would you want to ask me about it?' The first question that came back almost instantly was, 'Why?' A fair enough response, I suppose, and one I will hopefully address in the first few chapters to what led me towards becoming a co-parent. I will continue to intersperse and address the rest of their questions as I move through the chapters, using examples from my experience wherever possible. If you decide to do this yourself, please take notes as I would be keen to read it one day too. Platonic co-parenting can be an emotive subject and I have found people can have interesting, and sometimes extreme, opinions about it. This is all grist for the mill, of course. I hope you enjoy our journey through a relationship less ordinary.

The Art of Falling Apart

September 2011

Some days are more eventual than others. Some, we can look back at and see they were, in fact, turning points for the rest of our lives. The day I refer to here was an exceptionally sunny October afternoon in 2011. The launch day for a new charity I was starting in Brighton's glorious Stanmer Park. It was also two days away from moving into a new house with my partner, Miranda. A home we had been planning to have a family in. Something I had wanted for so many years. Miranda turned up unexpectedly at the park, which surprised me, as she should have been at work. She seemed anxious, avoiding eye contact and clutching a crumpled piece of notepaper. We sat down on a grassy verge in front of an old picturesque church, and with the sun beating down, Miranda read aloud from the scripted notes in front of her. Like someone reading a play on their first day of drama class. A play that turned out to be a tragedy, for I was being dumped. And with little in the way of a coherent explanation for her decision, she got into her car and I never saw her again.

For the previous 14 years leading up that tremendous day, I had been working as a social worker at a time of severe government cuts to public services. I had become crippled with stress and exhaustion, waking up in panic at 3 a.m. most days. On a cocktail of antidepressants and sleeping pills — like many other social workers in my office — we had become a hoard of white-collar zombies. Barely clawing our way through each day. I had craved a new job, but like any abusive relationship, social work had drained my confidence to such a low ebb I kept putting it off. The house that was to become our family home was near derelict when I bought it, and I had spent evenings and weekends, with little D.I.Y. know how, covered in grime and dust trying to renovate it.

Because I already had this shit-storm of a life, losing my relationship hit me hard. Really hard. Like a steam train. Transporting nuclear waste. It was the first time in my life I had felt broken and wasn't sure if I would ever fix myself. I spent the winter alone in the only furnished room in the house, with barking grief and billowing anxiety pouring out of me. I was only 42 years old, yet I felt like there was nothing left to live for. Heavy stuff, hey? Don't worry, this story gets so much better from here on in. Some parts might even make you laugh.

Voodoo Lady

March 2012

Spring had arrived. I had made it through the winter, just. It had been a season spent stretched out on my sofa, lost in a futile attempt at soul searching, surviving on a diet of pot noodles and digestive biscuits. By the time March arrived, I had reached peak slob. I was, however, feeling a little more emotionally robust by this time, I'm happy to say.

Part of me had always known it wasn't right with Miranda. Separation would have been inevitable, eventually. So why had this hit me so hard? It was a walk along Brighton seafront on a bitter overcast January afternoon when I had an insight into that. I realised it wasn't the loss of my relationship that I mourned so heavily, but the promise of becoming a parent. Where ever you might have read that men don't get broody. Don't believe the hype. Ever since a close friend's 5-year-old daughter threw her arms around me and screamed, 'I love you, uncle Nick!' I was about 35 then and I just knew I had to be a parent. As the years progressed, the yearning had grown stronger and stronger. So, what's a boy to do? Get off his backside and get dating, of course. And how was everyone doing that these days? By swiping right or left on their mobile phones. God help me.

So here I was, destined to go out dating with baby goggles on. What could possibly go wrong? The question I was asking myself was, 'how can you tell if someone wants a baby?' You can hardly slip that into a conversation on the first date. I thought about creating an Excel spreadsheet that organised dating schedules based on the Biodynamic moon calendar. Though if I'm honest, I'm not 100% sure of the science behind that method. My preferred option would be to steer the conversation (as subtly as possible) towards the subject of babies at every opportunity. I may pick up some clues that way. Fool proof, surely? It was a technique that wouldn't ever really get me anywhere, except with Karen, that was.

They say that your first online dating experience is the worst and I'll let you decide if that was true for me. I got chatting online with Karen, who seemed interesting, clever and funny. She was at a top university in London doing a PHD in a subject I couldn't even pronounce, which was a little intimidating. We hit it off after a chat on the phone as she was incredibly interesting and had a fantastic sense of humour. I agreed to travel up to London and meet her in the student bar of her university. When I arrived, I spotted her straight away. She actually looked like her profile photo. In fact, she was even more attractive in real life. The only alarming thing was that she was sitting at a table with four of her girlfriends, all wearing enormous smiles as I approached them. How awkward was this? They obviously all knew this was a date. It felt like I was about to audition for dragon's den. After half an hour of jilted conversation, wishing I could be anywhere else is in the known universe, Karen decided it was time for us to leave and go for a walk. Phew.

We found ourselves in a local park; we got some coffee and sat down by a lake. I was starting to relax and enjoy myself by this point, and as a double blessing, the sun had showed its face. Karen was talking about the failings of western philosophy, so I thought I'd chance my arm and try to impress her with my knowledge of existentialism (smooth). It took her around three minutes to realise I was faking it, at which point she decided to go for a thorough analysis of my last relationship. I felt coerced into recalling the car crash experience I'd had with Miranda the previous Autumn. A barrage of questions followed: Why do you think she left so suddenly? Did you mistreat her? Neglect her? What would you do differently next time? Intense for a first date, I felt, but I'm fairly open, so I did my best to answer her questions. I thought it was only fair, however, that I ask about her previous relationship. This was received about as warmly as inviting your neighbours round for a game of kiss chase during lock down. Clearly a one-way conversation. Despite this blip, we had a lovely day together. 5 p.m. arrived, and as I was thinking about leaving when she invited me back to her house for dinner. Really? On the first date? Who did she think I was? I'm not some dirty man-whore, you know. I value myself much more than that. I've got self-esteem. Absolutely no way.

As we were walking into her flat, she told me she cooked a mean vindaloo. I may well be weak willed, but at least I'll be well fed. It seemed to take a matter of minutes for Karen to transform her place into something reminiscent of a Barry White video. Candles, incense and soft music. It was almost as if this had been planned. Poppadoms and wine were served, and we sat at the dinner table regaling witty anecdotes about our gloriously sophisticated lives. How wonderfully cultured we appear until people get to know the seething mass of neurosis we really are. I decided now was the perfect time to hit her with my baby probing technique. Here's how I played it:

'You know you were asking about my ex earlier?'

Karen nodded.

'The reason we split up was that she decided, at the 11th hour, she didn't want kids.'

'Why the hell not?' she replied, munching on a poppadom.

'I really don't know. Not everyone wants kids, do they?'

'I can't wait to have a baby.' Karen swigged back her wine as if to cement this unshakeable statement of intent.

Bingo! (See, I told you I was smooth). But just as I was feeling this was someone I might be interested in, the conversation turned personal again. Very personal. The questions came thick and fast. What's the worst thing you have ever done? What are your faults? It was relentless, and it all felt a bit orchestrated. By this time, I'd had two glasses of Pinot Noir and I didn't feel like playing along. I told her I wasn't comfortable with the questions.

She tutted and stood up suddenly, knocking over her handbag that had been perched next to her chair. Its contents fanned out across the living room floor. One item took my attention above all the others, partly because it fell close to my feet but mainly because it was a rag dolly with pins sticking out of his head. (And no, it wasn't a pincushion) Alarm bells? yes, big ones. Bigger than the great bell of Dhammazedi. Before I could act, she had scooped up the dolly and scuttled off to the kitchen, shouting over her shoulder, 'I'll make us some coffee.' I was pretty freaked out, so I followed her into the kitchen and asked her what I felt was a legitimate question. 'Can you tell me what that rag doll is?' After a few minutes of banging about in her cupboards, she turned to face me. The conversation went like this.

'It's Richard.'

'Who is Richard?'

'My ex.'

'When did you split up?'

'6 years ago.'

'What did he do?'

'He left me. It makes me feel better when I stick pins in him.'

I'm sorry to say I also left. Karen was lovely, but I don't think she was completely in the right place for a relationship. As I walked down the street towards the tube station. The thought crossed my mind. *I hope I didn't upset her. What if she made a dolly for me?*

That was my interesting introduction to online dating, but I have to say I was undeterred. I wanted a child so badly I would persevere for another year. Even if it meant having pins stuck in my head. I was completely unaware at the time of what a monumentally bad idea this was. Few rules in life that are set in stone, but is wanting children the best motivation for seeking a romantic relationship? Would it be giving the relationship the best foundation for success? And what if it didn't work out? I could end up as a bitter co-parent. God forbid.

A Game of Two Halves

June 2013

I used to be the striker for a Buddhist football (soccer for my American friends) team. Our motto was 'fun over competitiveness.' I'd never experienced such violent anarchy in all my life. Whilst tucking into our post-match 'bring a dish to share' picnic, I had a chance conversation with a woman called Jenny who mentioned, casually, she was about to go 'halves on a baby with someone.' I almost choked on the home-made hummus. She had definitely got my attention. Intrigued, I asked if we could go for a herbal tea so she could tell me more about it.

Jenny told me she was to become a co-parent, albeit not a platonic one, in her case. She was in a relationship with another woman but had met a man that lived abroad who was to become the father of her child. Apparently, this alternative family structure had been commonplace in the LGBTQ communities for many years. I showed my ignorance by having a limited awareness of this. The term 'rainbow family' was first coined in the 1990s by an American sociologist named Daphne Simeon. It was during this time that she noticed that there were more diverse types of families than just the traditional nuclear family. Today, rainbow families are more popular than ever, as there are more people who identify as LGBTQ+ than ever before. The different types of rainbow families might include gay fathers, lesbian mothers, gay couples with children, transgender and intersex parents. Each type of family is unique and has its own characteristics.

The challenges that rainbow families face vary depending on their specific situation, but it is quite common for them to feel isolated, misunderstood, face discrimination, prejudice, and struggle to find support. This led us into talking about the relationships people we knew were having in Brighton, like polyamory, which is a form of consensual non-monogamy where people have more than one intimate relationship at the same time.

The more Jenny told me about the friends she had and their 'rainbow family' configurations, the more it fired my imagination. This was a new, exciting world of possibilities. Why wasn't platonic co-parenting more commonplace in the heterosexual world?

I walked home with my mind blown. My relationships had been positively vanilla in comparison. Maybe I needed to get a bit more adventurous. Maybe I could have an open relationship and co-parent? Why not? Who dictates what the rules should be? By the time I got home, I knew I was kidding myself. I'd last a week, if that. I get insecure if my partner's ex-boyfriend gets back in touch. Especially if he's better looking than me. (How is that possible I hear you ask? You really are too kind). My personality has two distinct sides. Psychologically, I'm Indiana Jones, emotionally I'm more like Scooby Doo. Something that has caused a modicum of dissonance at various points in my life. Alas, I run full steam ahead with a wonderfully fabulous idea and then once I'm doing it; I retreat into a dark corner and quietly shit myself. Co-Parenting was going to be no different.

I sat down and did a lot more research on this new alluring phenomenon. I realised that etched deep inside my emotional programming, this notion of a nuclear family was the benchmark I had been chasing my entire life. What was this volitional force driving me forward? The term "nuclear family" was first coined in 1947, and it described "a family group consisting solely of father, mother, and children." The question of who belongs in the nuclear family has always been a source of contention. Some argue that the children must be biological or full-blood relations, while others claim that stepchildren and adoptive children count too. This type of family became dominant in western culture. According to many historians, the church and theocratic states were a powerful force behind this. Christianity constantly promoted a stable family with a husband, wife, and children throughout most of its denominations. However, the origins of the nuclear family may be traced back to more than religion; many people also credit the industrial revolution. Over in the United States, the post-war baby boom of the 1950s and 60s had an impact as well, with a substantial increase in the number of young couples establishing families. Despite this social conditioning, things are slowly changing. It has always been traditional to consider marriage as a male-female union, the truth is that same-sex couples are becoming more and more frequent. Same-sex marriage being made legal in many western countries now has led to more non-heteronormative families.

I can't deny that the thought of finding my soul mate and being with her (until I am incontinent in a wheelchair) was romantic. But how common is it in practice? Or is it just an internalised fairy tale? On researching divorce rates over the last 40 years, I came across some quite sobering statistics. In the USA, for example. Couples in first marriages have a divorce rate of 42-45% which bumps up to 60% when moving onto second marriages. If you survive long enough to get married a third time, there is a 73% probability it will end in divorce.[1] The more you marry, the more likely it is to end in divorce. Also, given the fact the average divorce costs $12,900. It will cost you $38,700 for the privilege of 3 divorces. The phrase 'a glutton for punishment' comes to mind. Of all the statistics I waded through, possibly the most shocking was that 27% of divorced fathers in the U.S have no contact with their children.[2]

Over here in the U.K. the divorce rate has dipped and risen over the last 20 years. Between 2003 to 2009, however, the number of marriages declined, with fewer couples getting married. Regardless of these variables, 42% of all marriages end in divorce.[3] If these couples had children, they would automatically become co-parents. Possibly with lingering resentment and tension spilling over from the emotional wounds of their relationship. I reflected on what could be so wrong about entering into co-parenting intentionally? Without any emotional fall-out, two (or more) people focusing all their attention and affection on the well-being of their child?

Alongside the same-sex communities, I could see how co-parenting could be a very attractive proposition for certain types of people. Take, for example, someone who had grown up in a family marred by a messy divorce. The desire to not to subject their own children to the same fate may be enough to consider an alternative route. Or someone with very limiting health problems that may find supporting a child full-time too difficult to manage. What if someone is aromantic and simply doesn't desire a romantic relationship? How about people brought up in non-nuclear family structures? There are parts of Africa and Latin America where extended families, even polygamous, are the norm. Indigenous communities are another example - they have family models and cultures very different from ours. The Tojolabales, for instance, is a group that lives in the southeast of Mexico. They have a particular way of understanding the family: everyone is related to everyone because they belong to the same town. In this big household, each person has their own function and makes it possible for the community to move forward.

Health factors were definitely a consideration for me when reflecting on my parenting options. I had spent my twenties playing in various post punk bands and whilst I had a fantastic time, it left me with chronic tinnitus and hyperacusis (noise sensitivity). I often wondered how I would cope with the inevitable noise of especially a baby or young toddler. Perhaps co-parenting could be a perfect halfway house to help me manage this. Lost in google, I also stumbled across a co-parenting matching site called Modamily that looked very interesting. I signed up straight anyway. But surely, I couldn't do this and internet dating at the same time, could I? Of course, I could.

Choices, Choices

So, there I was, on two separate websites. One for a potential partner and the other for co-parent. How bohemian was I? Because of my total inability to decide (I'm Pisces), I had resigned myself to the philosophy that whatever was meant for me would come to me. A 'traditional' family had always been my first choice, though it felt that was becoming increasingly unlikely because of the time frames I had set myself. I didn't want to be an old dad (I was fairly knackered already). It was definitely time to look at the menu of family options and cast my net as wide as possible.

One of questions I was asked on the forum was, 'what were the qualities were you looking for in a co-parent?' I was well aware at the time this may be one of the most important decisions I would ever make. Luckily, I felt very clear on this from the start. I narrowed it down to three areas that would guide my choice:

1. *No romantic connection.*

I had a strong sense that if I was going to do this, I should stick to the concept of platonic co-parenting and choose someone there was no romantic chemistry with. I wanted to keep the entire process about the child. Any side agendas could only complicate matters and make things more complex to navigate. Even with this boundary in place, feelings, as you know, have a life of their own and rarely do what you tell them. There is always the chance of system malfunctions, which, as you will soon come to learn, is what happened to me.

2) *Emotional Intelligence.*

A quality that's always useful to have in a relationship, I find. How in touch with their feelings is this person? How able or willing are they to communicate them to me? Are they trusting, empathic and forgiving? Would we be able to resolve the inevitable disputes that would arise in a satisfactory way? No one is perfect, of course, and these qualities are always a work in progress. It's important to know if your co-parent has an interest in personal development. I believe this makes a big difference to the quality of your communication, relationship and, ultimately, your child's happiness.

3) *Compatible Value Systems*

This may sound obvious, but it's easy to overlook in the early stage. (I have met co-parents that have done this.) If one of you has strong vegetarian or vegan principles, how would you feel about your child being taken out for a hamburger on the weekends? Do you want to bring your child up bilingual? How do you feel about alternative schooling? Do you have religious or cultural expectations? The things that are most fundamental to who you are need to be addressed at this stage. how negotiable are they? These core principles all need to be clearly expressed, agreed, and written into your co-parenting agreement.

Even though I was apprehensive, but I grit my teeth and started going out and meeting potential co-parents. If I'm honest, before my first meeting, I had the fleeting thought. *What kind of wierdo am I about to meet?* This was interesting, as it showed that on some level, I obviously harboured some prejudice towards this alternative reality I was embracing. My preceding thought was *a weirdo like me, I suppose.* I found the process a bit like dating in some ways. For one, I instantly knew if someone wasn't right. It was a gut reaction. I knew I didn't want a romantic connection, but I definitely needed *a* connection. This person would become a very important figure in my life. We needed to form a relationship based on mutual respect and shared values.

The first person I met on the co-parent site, I felt I had a connection with, were actually two people. A lesbian couple, whom I developed a great affection for. They had all the emotional values and principles I was looking for and of course there were no romantic feelings between us because... do you really need me to spell that out? We decided we would have weekly meetings and go through some divorced couple co-parenting agreements we had found online. We wanted to discuss all the issues that we imagined might arise. Our discussions carried on for around six months, and it was really a valuable experience for me. It forced me to think about what exactly I was getting into and what I needed from it. I would learn later that perfect foresight is never an exact science, but by discussing (and writing down) what you agree, you can go a long way towards feeling secure in your co-parenting relationship. Our meetings were very productive, bringing up all kinds of things that had never even entered my head. I would say eighty percentage of what we spoke about I was in complete agreement with, but there were some lingering concerns I felt were non-negotiable. For example, there were certain religious conventions I wasn't comfortable with. It made me realise the importance of a secular upbringing for my chIld. Religion is fine, but I wanted it to be my child's choice, not mine. Also, I felt that however hard getting things working with one person would be, two would be a much harder dynamic to contend with. There would be so much more scope for disagreement. After six months, we all decided our partnership would not be compatible. We parted on good terms. I would remain forever grateful to them for having gone through this process with them.

At this point, I felt very clear about what I was looking for, which could only help with the next potential co-parent. This was a woman called Rae who was the first heterosexual woman I had met via Modamily. We met in a pub in Worthing and I instantly got the sense she was a good person. Principled, articulate and easy going. We agreed to meet again.

I didn't know at the time, but Rae would later become the mother of our child.

Co-Parenting Agreement

One question I got asked about the early stages of co-parenting was, 'How well do you get to know a person before planning to have a baby?' It's a good question. I remember an article I read on this issue declared in bold text, 'you must wait at least a year.' Which I felt was a little prescriptive. Because I'd waited so long to have a child, and now I'd found someone actually willing to be the mother of my offspring, the temptation was to jump straight in. However, as is usually the case, Rae was the wise and moderating influence on me. 'Seeing we have come this far', she said, 'why rush in and mess things up?'

What also later became apparent, if you want to get to know someone, a great place to start is by putting a co-parenting agreement together with them. Rae and I decided to meet weekly and go through all the aspects of an agreement to have a child together. Each week, we would look at a distinct set of questions and discuss how we felt about them. Subjects like: names, parental responsibility, education, child maintenance payments, parenting styles, discipline, custody (in case of death of both parents) screen time (that old classic) rules for future partners, health care, diet, child access and school holidays. We did this alongside some trips to the cinema and generally getting to know each other better. We both agreed giving some time to developing our friendship was going to be an important ingredient. This is was something Rae felt we didn't do enough of in the early days which she talks about later in this book. Our discussions felt relaxed and unforced considering what we were doing. I think Rae and I are quite pragmatic people. We both knew this was a perfectly reasonable solution to the place we both found ourselves in. Then one day, after about five months of discussions, we ran out of questions. *What comes next?* I remember thinking. When I am unsure about something, I usually write... until, I am sure. In this instance, I took to writing up our co-parenting agreement. When this was completed, I felt an elevated sense of achievement. So much so, I asked Rae if she would like to meet up for a walk in a local park.

We met and on what seemed to be the first sunny day in July. After a brief walk around a sparkling lake, we sat down on a grassy verge and ate sandwiches. I recall that there was barely a breeze. The trees were still. This brief moment of calm appeared to be the perfect opportunity to pop *the* question,

'Shall we have a baby then?'

Rae nodded, smiled and said, 'yeah sure thing.'

Who said romance was dead?

How important is it to form a co-parenting agreement? I believe it's imperative. Looking back at our agreement now, I realise there were a few topics we should really have discussed in more depth. This was a peril of not having much access to guidance when we started. Even without knowing how much support the law offers platonic co-parents, however, it always seemed intuitively right to discuss, agree and put everything in writing. For my side, the agreement made me feel held by the process. It is also a document you can refer back to should you feel like you ever lose your perspective on things. In later chapters you will learn that this is something I have had to do and how it helped me enormously. Alongside this, Rae and I have tried to build in regular check-ins to talk about how we are finding things. In the hustle and bustle of everyday life these are not as always as regular as we would choose, but we are both aware to make time for them when they are needed. I think they are enormously helpful in staying connected with each other, our current aims and our daughter's needs. It helps me to feel grounded and that I am contributing as effectively as I can. If I need to change things about myself or the way I go about things in certain situations, I am more than willing to do this, but I need to learn about my shortcomings first. That's where the check-in space is so important. I asked Dr. Lauren Brim, author of *The New American Family*, what she felt was important for co-parenting partnerships. This was her response:

"Issues will come up in your parenting and intense feelings will arise, so you want a space created where you personally and collectively, as co-parenting partners, can go to work through communication difficulties or disagreements."[4]

One thing we were unclear about was the amount of legal protection afforded to Platonic Co-Parenting. I assumed that our parenting agreement would offer us legal protection in the event of a dispute arising. It is, of course, never wise to assume anything. I thought it would be interesting to ask an attorney and a lawyer from both sides of the pond for their take on the subject. Thomas S. Gleeson Esq. an American attorney from Baby Legal Law Firm, was kind enough to give me his thoughts on the following question: How much support does the law in the USA currently give platonic co-parents?

First, I am a California attorney, and not familiar with the laws of all of the states outside of California. However, in general, there is no specific statutory support for co-parents. They should enter a co-parenting agreement, but this is a private agreement between parties and not enforceable per se. If a dispute arises, that requires going to court, this would be a custody case, like after a divorce, and the co-parenting agreement is treated as evidence, which a judge is likely to take into consideration when making a ruling.[5]

I also asked Emma Willing, a family lawyer at the British firm Mishcon de Reya LLP the question: *What would be your advice to anyone entering into a platonic co-parenting agreement?*

Whilst individuals having options to create families through non-traditional routes is undoubtedly positive, anyone considering entering into such an arrangement should do so on an informed basis. It is important for any party contemplating platonic co-parenting to do so with a full understanding of their potential future rights, responsibilities and obligations in respect to the child. Parties should consider entering into a co-parenting agreement. Although such agreements are not legally binding in England and Wales and cannot be enforced, the process of entering into a co-parenting agreement allows parties to carefully consider issues that may not have previously been discussed. Whilst many co-parenting relationships progress without issue, if a dispute does arise there can be difficult and complex issues for the parties involved to grapple with, often as a result of mismatched expectations at the outset. Therefore, it is important that arrangements are discussed between the parties at an early stage, if possible, with the benefit of legal advice.[6]

Should you be contemplating this path for yourself, taking the appropriate legal advice is obviously extremely wise. I've put a copy of our agreement at the back of this book for you to see. Baby Legal have also kindly agreed for me to share their list of issues to get you thinking about what you will need to include in your co-parenting agreement. Our co-parenting agreement begins with a declaration of our core values and life philosophy, which guided how we reached the decisions we came to for our child's well-being. Here is what we wrote:

- All decisions made should center around and be in the best interests of the child.

- The child will grow up in a liberal minded environment of love and acceptance.

- Any disagreements between any of the parents to be kept away from the child.

- For the parents to not speak ill of each other in front of the child.

• To never use or manipulate the child because of any disagreement.

• Consistency in child-rearing practices, we agree to keep regular contact with each other about our ongoing parenting practice.

• Don't make assumptions.

• Be true to yourself.

• Be impeccable with your word.

• Try to judge as little as possible.

• Continued growth and self-awareness.

• Live to eat, not eat to live.

• Trust yourself and you will know how to live (I'm sure this sounded good at the time, but I think we could have worded this differently).

• Acceptance of others and self-acceptance.

• Endeavor to practice patience.

Going through this process was an eye-opening experience, and it surprised me how easily our discussions had gone. I was expecting far more disagreement between us. Because the process was quite effortless; it cemented the fact that I was taking this journey with the right person. You can never be 100% sure, but I was sure as I could be. Because I had gone through this process once already, I already worked out most of what I wanted. For example, I was clear I wanted to have the rights and duties of parental responsibility. It can be a valuable use of your time to go through a practice run of putting a co-parenting agreement together with your most sceptical friend before you jump into the real thing.

I believe it is vitally important to get it all out there at this stage. Discuss everything on your mind and pin as much down as possible. Some things will invariably change, but you need a starting point for your discussions. It's also good to check in on your agreement every 6 months for the first few years. This helped me to feel more secure about the process, as well as feeling listened to. You may find issues pop up you weren't expecting when the baby comes. We did, which I will go into later. Luckily we have negotiated our obstacles, but I've heard of situations where this hasn't been the case. Why risk it? A co-parenting agreement is a conceptual process, and disembodied in some ways. When your beautiful baby comes along, it may redefine everything you thought you knew about the universe. For me, there was an awe-inspiring baby love explosion! (I know I'm dramatic, but I enjoy it). It's at this stage you may change how you feel about certain aspects of your co-parenting agreement. Buyer beware.

Party Time

I often argue with myself. I'm not strange. Okay, maybe a little, but it's mainly an attempt to keep my personality in check and be a presentable member of society. It often fails, but at least I'm trying. I recall one such conversation I had immediately after emailing a copy of our co-parenting agreement to Rae.

'We've got our co-parenting agreement in place. We'll start trying to get pregnant soon. Everything is going to plan!' I encouraged myself.

'Hold your horses, Einstein,' blurted out my rather belligerent inner critic. *'What about letting friends and family know about your eccentric little venture first?'*

'Oh, I forgot about that; do I have to?' I replied.

'Yes, you absolutely do,' demanded Les.

Just so you know, Les is the name I give to my inner critic. I think of him as an elderly, out of touch art critic who drinks too much wine. It helps me to not take him too seriously. See, I told you I'm not strange. I have to say, though, this was one of the rare occasions Les was actually right. It really was time to tell everyone.

I'm happy to say I have a liberal bunch of friends and family. Even so, I was anxious about how they would react to my news. I deliberated on various ways I could share this information. I seriously thought about announcing it as my Facebook status update and then going into hiding for a month. That may have been seen as the coward's way out though, so be brave, I thought, and get my parents out the way first.

I sat down in their front room with a cup of tea (all tough conversations must be accompanied by tea). The top of my hot beverage wobbled as my hand tremored slightly, 'I'm thinking... of doing platonic co-parenting.' I mumbled.

My mum looked bemused. 'What's that love?'

'It's something... a little different¾.'

'What is it?' Asked my dad before biting into a toasted crumpet (crumpets can be a hindrance to a tough conversation).

'It's when two people who aren't in a romantic relationship have a baby together,' I managed to reply.

A realisation swept across my mother's face. 'You're going to have a baby!?'

'Yes, but it's the way I'm doing it.'

'Sounds a little unusual, how will you¾.'

'Oh, do shut up Terry!' My mother cast a Darth Vader glare at my father across the living room. She then turned back to face me. 'So... you're definitely going to have a baby?'

'Yes.'

Half an hour later, after I had peeled my dear old mum off the ceiling, I realised this was going to be one of the biggest non-issues ever. The prospect of a grandchild trumped all other concerns. With me being in my forties and a single child, my parents understandably thought the baby ship had sailed. Suddenly, it was back in the harbour. I don't think my mum would have been all that bothered if I had said I was ordering a baby from the dark web. I joke, of course. When I asked her recently how she felt in the weeks after my announcement, this was her reply,

'When you first told me about your intention of becoming a co-parent I had very mixed feelings. On the one hand, it opened up a flood of emotions because of the possibility of becoming a grandparent which I very much wanted. On the other hand, I had feelings of trepidation of this unheard-of process of having a child with someone who you were not in a relationship with. After our many discussions however, I was able to come round to the idea. I realised how much care and planning you were putting into this and that you would not rush into anything unsuitable.'

Next up were my pals. This might be a tougher proposition. I tested the waters by telling two of my closest friends first. They were absolutely fine with it but they almost chewed my ears off with all the questions they asked me. There was no way I was going through that with everyone. I decided it would be better to announce it en masse to the rest of my buddies. I just had to wait for the right occasion. A week later I received an invitation to a great friend's 50th birthday party. Bingo! This would be the perfect occasion to hijack with my agenda (I bought him a rolling stones album as a birthday present, so please don't judge me too harshly).

On the evening of the party, I waited until my buddies were all a bit merry, then crept across the room to turn the music down. Their conversations muted, and they looked up at me expectantly as I stood there with what must have been a pained expression on my face. I'd had a couple of glasses of Dutch courage so hoped I could get through this without a massive panic attack. I cleared my throat and opened fire. 'If you could all just listen for a minute, please, I've got an announcement to make.' I paused as the sea of faces seemed to multiply before me. There was a judder in my chest, it felt like my heart was attempting to escape my rib cage. I'd obviously not had enough wine. The birthday boy looked over at me with a scrunched-up face, trying to work out if I was about to be a major buzz killer. A voice from the back of the room piped up. 'Quick as you like!'

I cleared my throat again. 'You know I was planning on having a baby with Miranda?' A few heads nearest me nodded politely in unison.

'Well, I'm going to have a baby, anyway.'

'Wonderful!' A good friend of mine Tina clapped her hands excitedly then stopped. 'But I thought you were single at the moment?'

'I am.' I paused for breath again. This wasn't going very well. Maybe the whole announcement thing had been a bad idea. The birthday boy screwed up his eyes and swigged on his beer, having obviously decided that this was indeed a major party downer. I rallied myself to carry on. 'I'm having a baby with the lady I've met on the internet.' That didn't really help my cause. The room went as quiet as a morgue. I should have written a speech and just read it out. *'Keep going Nick, you arse,'* Les my inner critic kindly interjected. 'It's something called platonic co-parenting... it's popular in America... it's a caring partnership between two people who want to have a child.'

I could see confusion flickering across my friends' faces. They resembled a shoal of guppies. They were all clearly wanting to say something encouraging but not sure what that could be. After a few more awkward moments, the voice from the back of the room concluded with a sensitive encapsulation of possibly what the entire room was thinking. 'So... does this mean you're going to have sex with her or not?' My friends are liberal, but unfortunately, not always that deep. The birthday boy breathed an audible sigh of relief and quickly turned the music back up. A few more glasses of wine later everyone took it in turns to hug and congratulate me so I suppose it didn't go too badly in the end.

Despite my fears, most of my friends and family turned out to be remarkably good about this alternative family idea. All apart from one, that is. A very close friend. A self-confessed liberal and champion of many human right's online petitions. He approached me at the end of the party, a bit worse for wear, with a troubled look in his eyes and asked me this. 'What impact will it have on your children, if they are not able to witness a loving relationship between their parents?' I found the question both annoying and upsetting in equal measure. But it had upset me for a reason. It was a valid point and also a question that needed to be addressed. I didn't respond to his question, instead left the party feeling extremely uneasy.

After a few days with this question whirling around in my head, I came up with my response to it. Better late than never. I appreciate we live in a world where there are, unconscious, socialised norms by which people judge each other. It's only when we choose to deconstruct and look at these so-called norms that they do not always hold up as making much sense. When my friend expressed his concern that my child would not witness a loving relationship between my co-parent and I. It left me wondering what he meant by a loving relationship? Does he mean a lack of care, respect, friendship, communication, affection? Or does he see a loving relationship as being synonymous with a romantic and/or sexual form of love? A person who identifies as aromantic experiences little or no romantic attraction in their relationships. Someone who identifies as asexual experiences a lack of sexual attraction towards others. It is possible for a person to possess both theses orientations. Are we to believe that experiencing aromantic or asexual traits limits a person's ability to love? I am sure certain both the aromantic and asexual communities would strongly refute this.

If you believe it is critical for your child to witness a romantic relationship between their parents, you have to be prepared for a 50/50 chance that your relationship will fail and that your child will also witness your relationship breakdown. It's the flip of a coin that can't be escaped. In the West at least, the statistics show us this is a reality. I'm sure platonic relationships fail too but I would prefer my odds in working through things from a place of friendship rather than the messy entanglement of emotional attachment.

The majority of our love narratives in the West have been influenced by the European writing traditions of the late 18th century, the period of Romanticism. Poets like Keats, Shelly, Byron and Blake transformed the utilitarian views of what love had been seen as and created a very alluring vision for us to aspire to. A vision that still permeates western culture today. Paintings, books and films have sold us a promise that our one true soulmate awaits us. We just have to find them. When we do, all our woes will disappear. The world before us will be transformed, it becomes our very destiny to find this person and have this profound experience. In the eyes of your soulmate, you will be completely perfect. They will see you and love you for everything you are. Words will barely need to be spoken.

I'm not sure about you, but this doesn't really conform to my experience of relationships. Maybe I haven't been on the right dating apps? I'm sure I'm not alone in this, though. The vision of Romanticism is exquisite, even intoxicating, yet however much I wish it were true, I believe it to be an unrealistic view of love to aspire to. Most people go through life clinging to this kind of vision regardless of the empirical evidence that their lives present them with. We experience Intense feelings for our lovers and certain aspects of romance have a part to play in our lives. I don't reject it completely – I'm not a cynic. In my view, however, defining an entire relationship around romance it is neither a healthy nor secure foundation. If there is one rule in life that does not change. It is that all things change. Feelings change, chemistry mutates. What do we do when this happens in our relationships?

This magical aspiration of the Romantics paves over the self-work that we need to do in our relationships. It fails to acknowledge our human imperfections. We nearly all have some form of trauma, neurosis or difficult emotional programming we have picked up since childhood. We need a view of relationships that makes it not only our responsibility but our duty to recognise and work on these damaged parts of ourselves. If we don't, how can we avoid this trauma and damage from showing up in the emotionally fraught waters of our relationships?

Love is personal and unique to each person. It ought not be defined by any conceptual, historical, cultural or political dogma. It doesn't need to be qualified by sex, romance or any other person's notion of how they love. I feel a relief to realise we can unhook ourselves from these socialised and unrealistic expectations of what love is. For me love is about caring, empathy, kindness and commitment. Relationships are something that take work and lots of compassion. I show my love by taking the time to listen, making a point of recognising and acknowledging my co-parent's qualities. By apologising when I make mistakes and by being willing to forgive and show that I care. If my child witnesses these qualities between her parents, we will have set an excellent example. This may not be a 'romantic' relationship, but it is a loving one.

I have found that the whole concept of platonic co-parenting can illicit often quite extreme judgments from people. It seems to trigger people for a variety of reasons that I will attempt to give my opinion on later. This needs to be a consideration if you are choosing this path for yourself. How are you with criticism? Are you okay are you with stepping away from the herd? One thing we have discovered however, is that co-parenting isn't actually very visible. From the outside, people often see it you as a divorced couple who have remained on good terms. We don't announce our family status at our child's school and no one ever asks. So, no none knows. Although now I have written a book about it, that's probably going to change. Me and my big mouth.

The day after the party, I spoke to Rae on the phone. We both decided we didn't want to wait any longer, and it was time to make a baby. We put a day in the diary for the following week and I said I'd look on Amazon for an insemination kit. Roll over you romantics, *this* is love in the twenty-first century.

Tall Hippies, Vitamins and Little Fishes

June 2014

To boost my fertility, not only did I take vitamins, but I also attended the popular Sussex Jack-in-the-Green festival (Wait, you did what?). For those who don't know, the Jack-in-the-Green is an old English folk tradition that celebrates May Day and the passing of Spring into Summer. An effigy of the Green Man covered in foliage and wearing a floral crown leads a procession through winding streets up onto a grassy hilltop. A day of dancing and merry-making ends with him being stripped of his foliage, which is then thrown into the expectant crowd of revelers. Legend has it that if you catch a leaf from the green man, you will be destined for good luck and fertility. Surely this was worth a go, wasn't it? It would be good fun if nothing else.

Unfortunately, as the effigy was being defoliated, I struggled to get anywhere close to the stage on which the ceremony was being performed. I am only 5 Foot 5 inches and in front of me were rows upon rows of the world's tallest hippies (it must be something to do with the Sussex air). I jumped as high as I was able, but the flying leaves were being snapped up high above my reach. I could see the Green Man had almost been completely torn apart, so with one last herculean effort, as the last sprig flew above my head, I leapt up with all my might and caught it. Victory! I was quite proud of myself and felt certain it would make a difference. But you can't take that seriously, can you? I hear you ask. It's just superstition and folklore, surely? Who knows? But don't worry, I carried on taking the vitamins.

Of the various ways to get pregnant, a physical technique must be the best (aka sexual intercourse). Unfortunately, Rae insisted we opted for an insemination kit. She said something about being 'appropriate'. How terribly British. I joke, of course. We both agreed it was the only path to take. Some co-parents choose intercourse and far be it from me to say how anyone should go about their journey. Rae and I felt that it would have risked blurring the boundaries from stage one. Building trust and a firm foundation in what we were doing was going to be vital, and like any relationship, it would take time. We didn't want to do anything to jeopardize that by bringing potential romantic feelings into the picture. Our big night had arrived and so had our insemination kit. The kit we ordered had a thin tubing that attached to the end of the syringe to get the little fishes up as high as possible (I hope I'm not losing you with the science here). After everything had been sterilised and was ready to go, the next step in our foolproof alternative family formula was for me to go upstairs into the bathroom and work my magic. What you are about to read isn't something you will see in a co-parenting manual, lecture, or website (I know as I've looked). So, it pleases me to reveal this rare and much sought after wisdom. For the men reading, may you learn from my mistakes. For the women, may you witness the indignity of what male co-parents have to go through. Men suffer too.

My initial thought was how do you accurately ejaculate into a small plastic cup while sat on a cold tiled bathroom floor? I'd never considered the logistics before. One thing was for certain though, I knew this wasn't something I could do sitting on a toilet whilst keeping my dignity. For my first attempt, I leant one elbow directly onto the floor tiles, dropped my trousers round my knees and stoutly began my business. This was a classic rookie mistake. It took all of around fifteen seconds for the pain to sear up my elbow and my backside to go numb. Both these afflictions were enough to erode any semblance of eroticism I'd mustered up. Friends have asked how I got aroused in that situation. I replied with, 'patriotic thoughts of mother England.' That said, it's been my only sexual experience where it's been useful not to think about Margaret Thatcher (I hope you understand that joke).

I sat back up to replan my strategy. I had the idea to lay a thick towel on the floor with a rolled-up dressing gown for my elbow (This actually belonged to my house mate Linda, so I hope she's not reading this). Now I was getting somewhere, I reconvened. This time I was a little too enthusiastic, however, and as I was reaching my crescendo, I grabbed the tub only to find my body angles were all wrong. To my horror, I missed my target and glazed my bathroom floor tiles instead. This wasn't going well.

Half an hour later, stressed but undefeated (tenacity has always been my strong point). I tried again and I'm pleased to report it was third time lucky. I had managed a meagre donation. (In case you are wondering, I discovered kneeling improves accuracy. So now you know. There's no need to write in with your gratitude). I realise I could have just gone to my bedroom, but the bathroom seemed more clinical and appropriate. Don't ask me why.

Rae informs me that her side of the process was as equally fraught with accident and incident. The hidden cameras I had set up seemed to confirm that (Rae, I promise you, that is a joke). We knew we had a zero chance of success; we had gone about nearly everything in the wrong way. But we had a great laugh, and if you can't laugh in a situation like that, when can you? Do you want to know something even more funny? Four weeks later, we found out Rae was pregnant.

Waiting 9 Months

October 2014

If I'm honest, after having got this far, with all the effort and emotional upheaval, it was a bit of a bummer having to wait nine months for our baby to arrive. What were we supposed to do in the meantime? I was soon to realise it was a few things, and I got some of them wrong. It would obviously be important to meet each other's friends and family. This was almost like a conventional relationship, almost. Looking back, I realise that these were our first steps out as 'platonic co-parents' and there was an emotional recognition developing that this was going to feel quite different from my usual relationships. I must admit to being anxious about meeting Rae's family and friends. I suppose, like with my friends and family, I feared they would not accept what we were doing. First, I met Rae's family. I'm happy to say her brother, mother, niece and nephew were all friendly towards me. Phew, that was one hurdle out of the way. Next were Rae's friends. All of which seemed good people and -on the face of it- fine with what we were doing. No drama so far. Then, just as I thought this was going to be easy, this happened. Rae and I were invited around to some friends of hers who I felt an instant affinity with. They cooked my favourite meal and gave me wine, which is rarely a good idea. We laughed at each other's anecdotes. It was all going so well. Right until I launched into my story of seeing a spaceship in the Qatari desert when I was 12 years old (*'What now!?'* I can hear you say). Well, I grew up in the middle east and once I actually saw a spaceship. (That's all I'm going to tell you I'm afraid. I would elaborate further, but it's not exactly relevant). The point being, I think I may have relaxed a bit too much in these good people's company. I will always remember the look of abject horror in Rae's eyes, 'what I have let myself in for,' they seemed to say.

A few months later, when I had met most of Rae's significant others (and just about passed muster), there was a few months' lull. This was where I messed up. I should have been keeping in better contact with Rae. I think I got a bit lost at this stage. Rae has since divulged to me that my sporadic communication upset her during this time because she felt we should have been putting more effort into developing our friendship. She was, of course, correct. I'm not sure what I was thinking. This was all so new to me, and I wasn't sure of my role yet. I didn't want to be pushy or smothering, but I think I went too far the other way. Our communication wasn't what it was today. I was trying to act cool and groovy, but the truth was an anxious side of me had raised its head and I wasn't sure how to respond. We will explore this more in the coming chapters. Building our friendship was something we had both identified in our co-parenting agreement as being important to us and the vision we had for our child. Another reminder of the importance of having an agreement in place (and reading it from time to time to remind yourself). What lesson could I take away from this? I should have asked Rae what she needed from me instead of trying to work it out on my own. If I could live this moment again, that is what I would do. I think it's a fairly good principle for co-parenting in general. If you aren't sure, ask.

Not long after this period, I received a letter in the post with the opening sentence, 'You have a confirmed place on our NCT Signature Antenatal Course beginning the 2nd December 2014.' I loathe formal training courses. They nearly always trigger social anxiety in me. The one saving grace on this occasion was that it was being set in a family home. So at least they spared us the sterile hospital setting. I have a clear memory of sitting in the opening circle when they do that round of introductions. Apart from it being possibly the thing I hate most about human existence. I felt especially awkward on this occasion. Rae and I had decided we would not keep what we were doing a secret. But as I sat there, I realised I didn't know if Rae had said anything about our relationship to the instructor? Did everyone in the room know? It was the first time I was aware of being concerned about the judgement of others. My heart was beating fast as I awaited my turn to introduce myself and Rae. Why does it seem like the person right before you is talking for about two months? He was a very tall, rotund man called Jeremy, who wore round spectacles and was sporting an out-of-control beard that resembled a rhododendron.

'Tabitha and I...' Jeremy took hold of his wife's hand and stared down adoringly into her eyes. Tabitha looked distinctly uneasy. He continued, 'we have been trying to get pregnant for three years now and it was a miracle it happened.'

He said something like that. To be honest, I was too anxious to concentrate. My throat felt like sandpaper, and I could feel the moisture pooling in the palms of my hands. By the time Jeremy finally shut his cake hole, my heart was slamming itself against my rib cage. All eyes in the room had now turned on us.

What the hell am I supposed to say? Okay, let's go with this.

'Hi everyone, we are Nick and Rae. We're not actually a couple, but we've got a great story about insemination kits if anyone's interested?'

Part of me wishes I had said that, but the reality was I spluttered something about how happy I felt about becoming a dad. I asked Rae about her memories of the antenatal class and she told me she felt awkward about the couple's massage session we had to join in with. On reflection, this was the first time that we'd had any physical contact and here we were massaging each other in front of a room full of people. What seemed normal to everyone else was the opposite for us. I felt equally uncomfortable about the breastfeeding demonstration. I still can't help feeling it would have been better if Rae had volunteered for that rather than me.

Joking aside, this is an obvious example of how mainstream health courses gear themselves towards conventional relationships. It was one of the few moments that I have felt self-conscious about what we were doing. This was presumably my outdated social conditioning popping up and trying to shame me. It didn't work though, as, alongside experiencing a sense of not fitting in, I felt an even greater desire of not wanting to.

Boys Don't Cry

9th March 2015

We found ourselves nine months pregnant. I say we, because at the time it definitely looked like Rae was carrying the lion's share of the burden. The hospital allowed us to have one other person in the room when Rae was giving birth. I initially had it in my mind that it would be me, but Rae decided it would be more relaxing for her to have an old friend be with her. It would also spare her the indignity of having me staring at her lady parts. I think that's fair enough. Rae enlisted the kind support of Margaret, a strong and caring woman who agreed to sit with her during the birth. I would chew my fingernails in the waiting room.

Rae was nearly 43 at this point and because of this, the medical team at the hospital had wanted to induce the birth two weeks early. Their rationale was because of the potential health risks to older women. Rae decided she wasn't comfortable with this, however, and opted to hang on and go to term. After going a couple of days past this deadline, however, the hospital became much more insistent they wanted to induce the birth. Into hospital Rae went for what was to become a very uncomfortable five days. For the first three days, the doctors tried three times to induce the birth without success. Alongside this and the constant monitoring, Rae got absolutely no sleep and was becoming increasingly stressed by the experience. The medical team then announced they would break Rae's waters to bring on the birth. This process had a negative effect on our baby, though, whose heartbeat became irregular. Because Rae could hear this on the monitor, it was very distressing for her and her own blood pressure rose sky-high, prompting the doctor to perform an emergency caesarean. This was in the early hours of her fourth morning in the hospital. It was a very difficult and upsetting experience for Rae.

Earlier that evening, before Rae had gone through the intervention, we assumed (incorrectly) it was unlikely our baby was going to arrive that evening. As I'd been hanging around the waiting room all day, I went back to Rae's house to get some sleep. The next thing I knew, the phone was ringing early on the 9th of March. It was Rae. She said the most wonderful words anyone has ever said to me, 'you have a beautiful baby daughter!' I ran to the hospital faster than the speed of light or as fast as the decrepit rust bucket of a bus could amble through the Sussex countryside. Some forty minutes later, I was staring up at the glaring windows of the hospital, beaming out of the murky morning sky like an open star cluster. *What new life was awaiting me inside?* I thought to myself.

I had read how hard it can be for fathers -and indeed some mothers- to connect with their newborn babies. In the build-up to the birth, it was hard not to be concerned this might happen to me. My worry was misplaced though, as when Rae handed my daughter to me, it was like being hit by a love avalanche. Every atom in my being became brighter. Every fibre, more alive. We named her Milly, and she was the most delightful little pixie, all wrapped up in one of those pink hospital blankets. I strode up and down the corridor with her a few times, introducing myself, 'hello I'm your father. Don't give me any attitude and we'll get along just fine.' Milly's deep brown eyes stared up at me and glistened. She was obviously expressing her deep gratitude for having me as her parent. When Milly was 6, I relayed this experience to her, and she told me she was actually thinking, *are you the only dad available?* Bless her. With all the emotion and the buzz of the hospital environment, I started feeling a little dizzy. I needed fresh air. I handed Milly back to Rae and fled to find a cafe across the road. Luckily, it was deserted. I bought a coffee, sat down in the corner and wept for half an hour. It was a joyous tsunami of tears accompanied by a geyser of unrelenting snot (and Rae thought she'd had a difficult few days).

Baby Love Haze

April 2015

In chapter five, I told you one of the key pillars of my decision-making process was that I wanted to choose someone I had no romantic connection with. I also told you that your rational planning about co-parenting may be subject to change. In my case, something definitely changed. Milly was born. My daughter's birth was such an all-encompassing love explosion for me, my entire world turned upside down. I want to share with you an experience that completely caught me unawares. It was something our co-parenting agreement could not have foreseen.

The only way I can describe this incident is as a kind of love transference. The psychotherapists among you may disagree, but for want of a better term, this is what I will call it. Two weeks after Milly was born, I went for my weekly visit to see her. We were all sitting in the front room with Rae cradling our daughter in her arms. As we sat chatting, I stared blissfully at Milly. It was as if there was a glowing aura surrounding her. Suddenly, a curious thing happened. The divide between Milly and Rae dissolved. The aura was now encircling Rae as well. Wow, I didn't see that coming. In my endorphin addled brain, however, it all seemed to make perfect sense. I found myself wrestling with an existential conundrum. *If I love this little being with all my heart, and this little being was once part of this other being. Then maybe, I'm also in love with that being?* It was enough to give Plato a migraine. I went home and stewed on this unexpected revelation. The dilemma spun around my mind for a couple of weeks until I eventually plucked up enough courage to say something. Sat in Rae's living room again, during a discussion about disposable nappies, I spluttered out the following, 'Do you think we could make a traditional family?' What a thing to drop on Rae after everything we had planned and agreed. I have to hand it to her though. She dealt with it in the most unfazed fashion possible. She just looked at me, smiled and said, 'shall we just stick with the program?' I nodded and replied, 'yes, of course.' We then finished our discussion on disposable nappies.

I was disappointed at the time but after only a few days of reflection, I realised Rae was right. She had helped me navigate my way out of a baby love haze, with a big serving of compassion. I think the lesson here is that love spills out in ways that we may not predict. Especially when it's the love for your child. A love so strong it could move mountains. This is not the only time that Rae has been a grounding influence on me. My tendency, at times, can be to get overexcited and overly emotional. I blame these character aspects on being a Pisces and absolutely nothing to do with neurotic self-doubt.

There is some interesting research by psychologist Elizabeth Gould and her colleagues at Princeton University that looked at how becoming a dad changes a man's brain.[7] For women, it is pregnancy, childbirth and breastfeeding that cause hormonal changes. The research discovered that when men become fathers, they can experience a hormonal shift and develop increased levels of oestrogen, oxytocin, prolactin, and glucocorticoids. According to the researchers, dads who have stronger bonds with their children show higher levels of oxytocin. It is believed the father can also be affected neurobiologically because of the role he adopts in fatherhood. His brain can develop new neurons following the birth of his child, (at least in animal studies). The scientists believe this occurs as a result of the level of environmental richness brought on by a child in a father's life, or the extra dimension a child brings to the parental relationship.

So maybe my experience was because of some hormonal overload or a blip in the rewiring of my neural pathways? Or was it a kind of transference or love overspill? Whatever the case, it is helpful to know that this could happen in your co-parent planning journey. And it if it does, it may be prudent to sit with the feeling and give it some time. You might find your emotional defaults reset themselves given time. As my Cub Scout Leader, Akela, used to tell me, 'forewarned is forearmed.' Although I have to admit, I was cautious about taking his advice. He was a fully grown man who spent the weekends running around our local woods wearing knee-length socks, tight fitting shorts and shouting 'Dib dib dib, dob dob dob.' But hey, who am I to tell you what's normal?

Reality Bites

July 2015

Earlier in the book, I told you that my personality has two conflicting sides. The brave entrepreneur that schemes world domination, closely followed by his anxious alter-ego, who quickly finds himself of his depth. It was round about this point in the proceedings that I started getting a little anxious. And when I say a little anxious, I actually mean panic. The enormity of what I was doing had hit home. This was no longer a conceptual realm of 'how wonderful it will be to be a daddy.' This was swirling in the overwhelming emotion of my daughter's birth. Feeling increasingly vulnerable at every turn, emotional hijack became a daily occurrence. With hindsight, I'm sure that the intensity of the experience caused my inner wounds to raise their ugly heads, and I just didn't know how to cope with it. I also felt guilty because it was Rae that was getting the sleepless nights and had most of the work to do. I did everything I could to support her and try to adapt as best I could to my new role. Knowing it wouldn't help Rae, I tried to suffer in silence. It was my stuff after all. I'm not sure however, I was always good at doing that.

Nothing could have prepared me for the emotional deluge I experienced in becoming a parent. Having chosen to become a platonic co-parent seemed to add to that dynamic. My major fear was, *what happens if things go wrong between Rae and I? What I if I could no longer see Milly?* The thought was unbearable and tormenting in equal measure. Rae took on this all-powerful leviathan type role which seemed to dictate every move I made with Milly. This, of course, was purely a mirage from a fearful mind. But because of my emotional state, it seemed all too real. I noticed a pattern in how I was responding to Rae. An issue would arise and my reaction to it would be far too disproportionate. I could feel winded by a simple word out of place. And given that my co-parent hardly slept through the night for the first 4 years, this was a rife breeding ground for misunderstanding between us. God only knows what Rae must have thought of how I was responding to her at that early stage. I think we are both naturally cautious people and as we still didn't know each other that well, we hadn't yet built a solid trust between us. Looking back, it's not surprising this kind of thing came up for me. I couldn't have embarked on a more emotionally charged journey together, could I? With little in the way of a blueprint to follow, I sometimes felt like we were on a ship sailing into the fog, without a compass.

Our first (and luckily only) major test so far, arrived around this time. We had a difficulty come up around Milly's surname. In our co-parenting agreement, we had decided we would opt for a double-barrelled surname. However, after Milly's birth, Rae found she was no longer comfortable with this idea. I could see it was really bothering her. We found ourselves faced with a dilemma. Whose surname would Milly take? It was an issue that we both found very triggering at this early stage in our journey. For me, this issue became wrapped up with the notion of identity. I also believe It was linked to my fear that something might go wrong and I could get excluded. So, in my anxious thinking to give my name away, felt like too big a concession to make. The mother-child bond is so strong for the first few years even men that are living with their partners can feel on the outside of things. I think there can be a perception that fathers can appear distant or disinterested, but this could, for some, be a defensive response to that dynamic. Luckily, even at the time, I knew this insecurity stemmed from my emotional makeup. Not that knowing that made it any easier, but it gave me a course of action. Which was what any self-respecting person should do in this situation and that's taking out a bank loan.... to pay for therapy. Or rather, some more therapy. I could almost hear my therapist's thoughts as I entered the room. *Dear Lord, not you again, Nick.*

Therapy was the best gift I could have given myself, it helped me immeasurably. And with this, we hit upon an important point regarding this family choice. Having come this far, It is now my conviction that, for the most successful outcome, platonic co-parenting ought to be a journey in self-development. I'm not saying this has to involve a psychotherapist, but it's useful to have some kind of personal development plan that provides you with insight into what makes you tick. Particularly regarding your own relationship attachment patterns. Interested to explore more on this topic, I asked Thomas Larkin, a very established integrative psychotherapist based in Dublin, for his opinion. This was his response to the following question: What's your view on the role of platonic co-parenting in the light of high divorce rates and changing relationships in modern day society?

'John Bowlby's attachment theory is a wonderful indicator of how healthy, or not, our relationship style is. It doesn't matter how many years pass, the attachment style we have remains the same, unless we spend some time doing our own therapy. Fortunately, in this modern time, therapy is much more available than it ever was in humanity's history and it needs to be availed of by all. In terms of platonic co-parenting, fundamentally, if the relationship between the parents is very loose, this will impact the child. Children work off the relationship the parents have with themselves and each other. When the parental relationship is distant, the child will learn this distance. For me, regarding platonic co-parenting, both sides would have to look at what is happening for them in terms of relationships in their own therapy before they get into this agreement. Otherwise, it can be like building a house without the foundations in place.'[8]

I found that my family choice became an opportunity to not only work on myself but also develop my self-awareness, emotional intelligence and communication skills. I have found this was something that would help both my relationship with Rae, and my capacity to parent well. Rae and I didn't resolve the surname issue straight away, but we kept on talking and having regular check-ins. We were in a stalemate, but remained compassionate to each other's point of view. Eventually; we found a solution. Which was to give our daughter a unique surname and change our names to match. We could both live with this. Although the experience was unpleasant for us, I now see it as a testament to our ability to resolve difficulty through effective communication.

Like with any relationship, there will always be difficulties to navigate. It would be unrealistic to expect otherwise. In the early difficulties, lies an opportunity to grow trust and build a culture of understanding in your relationship. One of the core values in our co-parenting agreement was to always base our decisions on what is best for our daughter. We have both been very good at being guided by this principle and it can make the path forward seem much clearer in moments like this. The irony is, recently, Milly has decided, on her own accord, to change her name anyway.

After the first year, with the aid of therapy, I habituated to our situation and felt much more relaxed. I was no longer being triggered in the same way and my trust in Rae grew stronger and stronger, along with our communication. My one anchor in all this was the knowledge of how good a person Rae was. She is one of the most principled and compassionate women I have ever met. I have always had nothing but respect for her, regardless of the conflicting emotions of that first year. This highlights the importance of the qualities you search for in a co-parent. If you are looking for a co-parent, get clear on the values you want embodied in your relationship and may you choose wisely.

Abstract Jazz

February 2016

If you haven't tried it, dating when you have a baby is a joyous experience. Particularly when you are a platonic co-parent. Friends advised me at the time not to mention my 'interesting' family arrangement, but I'm not very good at keeping secrets (you may have noticed). After three weeks of sending out messages trying to convince women I was fun and interesting, someone eventually agreed to a date with me. Anabela was her name, and she had the most wonderful smile. More importantly, her pictures revealed a handbag that was nowhere near big enough for a voodoo dolly.

We met on the calming backdrop of Brighton seafront, which was lit up by some rare winter sun. Seagulls hovered on a gentle easterly breeze and foamy waves caressed the shoreline. After the initial awkward greeting, followed by the mandatory chat about the weather, we started a stroll along the promenade and a conversation about the merits of living in such a cultural city. Anabela revealed she was passionate about abstract jazz. I smiled and nodded politely, deciding it was best not to reveal the fact that I would rather eat fresh manure than subject my ear drums to such a weird pandemonium. We walked past a playground and luckily our conversation deviated onto the subject of children. Anabela told me she had a five-year-old. I thought it was only fair to tell her I had a baby. I wasn't prepared for the ensuing conversation. This is how it went.

'Didn't it work out with the mum then?' Asked Anabela, eyebrows raised.

Unsure how to respond, I opted for honesty. 'It worked out well, actually.'

'You mean you are still sleeping together?' Her eyebrows almost touched her hairline.

'No, we've never slept together.'

Anabela stopped and looked directly into my eyes. 'Are you messing with me?'

And this was how I found myself forced into an explanation of my lifestyle choice. I explained that Rae and I are two people that had met, formed a friendship with the intention of becoming parents in a platonic relationship.

At first, there was no response. Anabela continued walking, her raised eyebrows had been replaced by a furrowed brow. She eventually piped up, 'so you went with artificial insemination?'

'An insemination kit.' I replied.

'Why wouldn't you just go the natural route?'

'Because we weren't in a romantic relationship.'

Anabela grunted dismissively. 'That's a bit weird, isn't it?'

'You mean different, don't you?' I replied.

'No, I mean weird.'

'Like abstract Jazz you mean?' It was a cheap shot, but like I said, I was unprepared.

Anabela was visibly pissed off now. My stomach was churning. We continued to walk in silence for a few minutes. I tried to calm myself by listening to the waves before asking her. 'Divorced couples are also platonic co-parents, are they weird too?'

She opened her mouth to respond, but found no words. My forced explanation had now turned into a justification. I didn't have to play ball, of course, but I felt insulted and I knew my family choice was not something that I needed to hide or be ashamed of.

It turns out Anabela wasn't done though. 'I'd rather get pregnant from a fling than do that!'

Rarely am I gob smacked, but my only achievable response to this was to leave. I made my excuses and headed home under a cloud of rumination. The rare winter sun had dissipated. My head was spinning. *How could casual sex with a random stranger be preferable to building a thoughtful and caring family with a friend? Did I miss a lecture somewhere along the line?* By the time I got home I had a throbbing headache.

I had more dating experiences like this and I'd be lying if I told you it didn't dent my confidence. I will look at why I believe this subject is so triggering for people in the next chapter, but the question that troubled me the most at the time was; Is this going to prevent me from having a relationship? I really didn't know at that stage; all I could do was carry on dating.

What Are You Going on About?

If there is such a thing as a good marriage, it is because it resembles friendship rather than love. Michel de Montaigne, 16th century philosopher. [9]

Doing things differently is bound to turn some people's heads. Anything that upsets the apple-cart will come under fire. Even though, looking at the UK and US divorce statistics, one could deduce the nuclear family apple-cart is already quite upset. Regardless of this, if you choose platonic co-parenting as a family choice there is a high probability you will meet some criticism along the way. You shouldn't feel the need to justify your life choices to anyone, of course, especially when some opinions are ill-informed and antagonistic. Prejudice, like my waistline, seems to increase year-on-year. Our communities are becoming more and more polarized, it seems. In the UK, there was a dramatic rise in homophobic and transphobic hate crimes in 2021, the highest number of the last three years.[10] It's a similar picture in the USA.[11]

For some reason, I have always gone against the norms of society (whether consciously or unconsciously). Maybe it was coming of age in the aftermath of the late 70s punk scene, or maybe I just like being awkward. I'm never more animated than in a late-night conversation with friends over a bottle of wine ab
out subverting society's dominant paradigms. The problem is, it's very hard to escape the deep emotional underpinnings of our socialisation. From a very early age, internal programming comes to us via the media,

family, education and our culture's religious leaning. As we get older, whether we believe in these values or not, they can't help but have an effect on us.

As platonic co-parents, we need to find the resolve to rise above the haters and trust our conviction in following a path that has meaning for us. Even if it is less travelled. The problem can be that people love telling you, *their* opinions. I get faced with a decision. Let it go or challenge it. Most of the time I opt for the former, but sometimes I just can't accept being the passive recipient of prejudice. Especially when I haven't had enough caffeine that day.

Should you choose to engage, being informed and having thought about your responses comes in handy. Reflecting on the 'interesting debates' I have had, I've come across five core reasons that most people cite when objecting to platonic co-parenting. The first is our collective addiction to romantic love, which we looked at in chapter eight. I'll address the remaining four here by attempting to look at the belief systems that underpin them. I must add that some of these points could have essays written about them. All I can do is touch the surface with the time and space I have. It will hopefully be a useful starting point for consideration.

1) **Misunderstanding what platonic co-parenting is.**

I have found that there seems to be some difficulty around grasping what 'platonic co-parenting' 'is. There's little problem understanding the notion of co-parenting, as everyone knows at least one divorced couple. There's also no struggle with the notion of being platonic. Put them together however and you seem to get misfiring synapses. I have spent too many hours trying to explain it to scrunched up faces. So much so that I have been working on finding a way to summarise it as clearly as possible. Here goes:

Platonic co-parenting is the considered act of coming together with a friend to raise a child in a loving and caring support network.

What do you think? Does it do the job?

2) **Conflicting ideas about child welfare.**

I still have a few social worker friends, and I was out with some of them at a dinner party six months after Milly's birth. I was surrounded by four older women, grandparents themselves, who were former colleagues of mine. They were very interested to learn more about the 'fascinating' family structure I'd entered into. I explained that Milly's sleep had been very erratic, to which my four friends replied, 'How awful that must be,' and began offering a plethora of potential remedies that would correct the situation. It was all very empathic, right until I casually mentioned that Milly was co-sleeping with Rae. It was as if I had unwittingly set off a depth charge. I could sense a distinct grumbling as dentures started to grind. The mood was changing. The volume of these passionate views increased. Everyone was still trying to address the debate sensitively. After all, they were all social workers, liberal and understanding to a fault. Most of them had attended courses on non-violent communication, surely that would help them keep their cool? About one minute later there was a raging argument. Accusations were flying around the room over what responsibilities a mother should and shouldn't have and how stupid the other one was for taking the position they had. It was loud, embarrassing, and I felt extremely uncomfortable. I wanted them all to shut up and leave me alone.

People are passionate about child welfare, and so they should be. Any culture or society that doesn't have strong convictions, laws and protections regarding child welfare must be damaged. The trouble is, people can have very conflicting ideas about what is best for their children, and often, other people's children. Keep in mind, my unruly gaggle of social workers all had very similar politics, stemmed from the same culture and a common religion.

What happens in our multicultural societies where different belief systems and religions collide? Take, for example, the controversy around male child circumcision. A practice that is seen by some as having health and religious benefits, while others see it as a form of genital mutilation. All sides are passionate about their beliefs and able to construct convincing arguments to support their position. But who is right? And who decides?

One argument used against non-heteronormative families is that children need a traditional family model for healthy development; that is, a father and a mother. However, several studies point to the contrary. Research from *The New England Journal of Medicine* reports no differences in the mental health or cognitive development of 25-year-olds who grew up in same-parent families compared with a group of the same age who grew up in heterosexual-couple households.[12]

A study published in the *Medical Journal of Australia* reported the same results with one difference: Australian children who grew up in same-parent households received better quality parenting and showed greater flexibility about gender roles, sexual diversity, and different types of families.[13] Although the stigma of the children of these couples continues in multiple social circles, as the world moves forward and progresses, families that break away from the traditional structure will become even more common. Maybe the times really are changing.

3) Morality.

He's only taking on morality now, who does he think he is? I can hear your thoughts from here. I know this is a Moby Dick of a subject and alas I can only give you a shrimp's perspective. But it is an informed perspective and shrimps should have rights too. I need to be clear on what I mean by 'morality'. Morality concerns itself with systems of values as well as principles of conduct. Contained within the values of these systems is a position on whether an action is seen as right or wrong. Morality can be used to enrich and safeguard our lives. It can also be used to judge and exclude people.

In 2021, during the heart of the pandemic, there was a reality TV show in the UK called *Strangers Making Babies* (of course the title wasn't meant to be provocative). In the show, prospective platonic co-parents met each other for dinner in a date-style set-up to see if they would be compatible in raising a child. It felt very familiar to me as I had been in those kinds of meetings myself all those years ago. Understandably, there were some interesting opinions voiced about the show on social media the following day. One post suggested this 'weird' family format was utterly irresponsible and bound to produce screwed up kids. Plenty of people made it very clear they thought this form of parenting was morally wrong.

Both in the US and UK, conservative new right thinking dominated family policy during the 1980s and 1990s. They believed that previous government policy had degraded the institution of the nuclear family. The welfare state, they argued, led to a culture of dependency on handouts, which in turn gave way to a proliferation of single parenting, crime and moral decline. In their opinion, government policy should consider the nuclear family as the only acceptable option for society to function effectively. This gave rise to the Conservative Party in the UK launching a campaign in 1993 called 'Back to Basics', which was an attempt to install good solid values to get every household to enact a lifestyle reminiscent of *Little House on the Prairie*. A campaign that was only slightly marred by reports of affairs, homosexuality and divorce within the Conservative Party itself.[14] I believe we are still experiencing the consequences of that government policy now; it has percolated through society as the paradigm for what the ideal family should be. It is also apparent to me that the remnants of Christian morality still permeate a lot our core values around notions of identity, marriage, welfare, dignity, human rights, and law. Whether we are always aware of it or not.

So how do we deal with being told we are doing something wrong or weird? I've had this accusation come at me, not just from people of a religious persuasion but those claiming to be secular humanists too. When I've been confronted with these accusations from people who claim to be secular, it strikes me they are operating from a fixed position of what is morally correct, which is implicitly the same as a god-created order of things, even if the god part isn't explicit anymore.

This realisation has made me a lot clearer around where I take my own ideas of morality. I value individual inquiry over unquestioned rule-following. My concern is not for some universal god-given law (whatever a person's definition of God is). My focus is current-day society, what I can see and hear with my own senses. Being aware of our value base is vital if we are to untangle ourselves from outdated moral codes. I want to be able to ask myself, 'What values would I like to embody in the world?' - 'How can I support myself and others with these values?' - 'How can I stay open enough to realise I might need to change my mind on something?'

In the West, for the most part, we champion free speech. So, I would defend anyone for the right to speak their mind. As an ex-philosophy student, I feel that open discussions about morality are important. It is a very fluid subject (anyone who has stepped in the same river twice can tell you; things are constantly changing). The basis of morality ought to be an ongoing debate. It visibly changes and evolves. Two good examples are women's right to vote and the legal position of homosexuality. In any moral debate I find it important to ask that person what their frame of reference is. What is the value system from which they make their judgments? Talking about what makes up a morally 'good' or 'bad' action with this knowledge can deliver a much more productive discussion. Rather than having someone recite unexamined dogma to you.

The best we can do is to hold a question mark over the views we hold. No matter what philosophy or religion guides us in life, we need to be open to the fact we may not hold all the answers to the complex questions of life. Like my battered old laptop from which I write this book, we too may occasionally need an update. If we ever end up having computer chips inserted into our brains, then maybe that is exactly how it will happen in the future - we'll click on the OS update, and away we go! Then when you are confronted with accusations of moral irregularity, all you will need to say is, 'I'm not arguing until you get your update.'

Far from being immoral, I would argue that platonic co-parenting sets a strong ethical standard in many ways. For one, it empowers women to make their own choices about the kind of relationship they want to have. This frees them from patriarchal marriage structures that have been oppressive for so very long. This can only enhance the rights and security of women as well as expand their education and employment opportunities by not being tied to fixed roles and duties. Co-parenting being more flexible can also provide the space for these opportunities. Platonic co-parenting is planned and considered. It is 100% child-focused. My experience is that it provides stability for a child. Having two parents who are actively involved in their lives can only make a child feel more secure and confident. This can help them build healthy relationships in the long run, which is obviously something that's very significant. I have also found that it encourages parents to work on themselves as well as improve their communication, thereby improving their chances of resolving conflicts that may arise in the future. Essentially it comes down to what we feel are the important ingredients to raising a child in a loving, supportive and secure way. For me, the shape or construction of a particular family is of little concern.

I asked Karen Bonnell, author of *The Co-Parenting Handbook*,[15] how she saw the challenges of intentional platonic co-parenting compared to those of co-parenting as a divorced couple? Karen kindly wrote me the following response:

When two adults embark on raising a child together – with all the commitments to that child's physical, emotional, and spiritual wholeness that ideally underpin healthy parenting – they are co-parenting. This isn't an optional relationship – but rather one that once initiated or claimed, is "until death do you part" from the point of view of the child's heart. Successful co-parenting can occur on any number of levels of engagement (parallel co-parenting all the way to highly integrated co-parenting). What's important is that both adults understand what's needed and develop the skills to implement successful co-parenting on behalf of their shared child.

4) Seeing the nuclear family as the 'normal' or superior form of family arrangement.

This thinking is a close relative of the moral argument and can show up in a much more subtle form. Statements like, 'that's strange', or, 'sounds a bit odd to me!' are common place. In my experience these words can be used with a smile and often aren't meant to be divisive. According to new right policy, there was only one type of family that could be considered normal. That would be the nuclear or traditional family. In their view, this family structure is a 'natural' result of fundamental biological differences between a man and a woman. They argued that alternatives to this family model, like lone parents for example, cannot provide sufficient primary socialisation for children because of a lack of a male role model. Often, crime statistics involving broken families are referenced to try to prove their case. This is a very complex dynamic which I don't believe can be reduced to a single factor but it's important to say that platonic co-parenting - even when parents live in separate homes - is not the same thing as a broken home. Alternative families are not broken homes. You may not be married, heterosexual or live in the same house, but this in no way implies that the way you relate is damaged in any way. For platonic co-parents it is closer to a model of extended families that existed prior to the nuclear family. Milly has multiple family support networks across her two households. One of her homes is in the countryside, the other by the sea.

It's also important to stress that today the West has fewer nuclear families than ever before. The proportion of nuclear family households decreased by half between 1970 and 2012. A census showed that a mere 13% of all households in the 1960s were single-person homes. By 2018, this percentage had increased to 28 per cent. Family statistics give us an interesting picture because they show more diversity in family structures than you would suspect. According to *America Progress*, today only 69% of children live with married, heterosexual parents.[16] This is partly because of the growing number of LGBT families with children. They look after between 2 million and 2.8 million children worldwide. 24% account for female same-sex couples and 11% for male same-sex couples. These statistics would imply a growing divergence from the traditional nuclear family model. Is a reason for this shift due to the nuclear family model not meeting everybody's needs?

Ulrich Beck, the German sociologist, argued that a new type of family, which varies according to the members' expectations, has become normal. Beck called it the 'negotiated family'. Historian and sociologist Jeffrey Weeks argued that the changing family type results from the movement of personal sexual ethics from religious traditions. As a result of this secularization, sexual and family diversity are becoming increasingly accepted.

When I dyed my hair blue at the age of 18, my nan got quite upset about it, and in a heated exchange confronted me with, 'Why can't you just be normal like Kevin next door?' I never knew Kevin, but I found out years later he had left his wife and had sex reassignment surgery. While I find that perfectly normal, it would probably have turned my nan's hair blue. It's funny how life works isn't it?

Many people are so fixed in their views of what a family should look like that if you opt for this family choice, you may meet some judgement. I have found deconstructing these judgements both interesting and useful, especially when you see the flimsy suppositions they are sometimes built upon. When Rae and I stand in the playground after school, people know we are Milly's parents. They also know we aren't together. They all assume we were once together and are now just ordinary co-parents. The rare kind that stays friends. All the other parents are good towards us. Would their opinions change if they knew we had never been a couple? Would it be the fact we hadn't had a romantic or intimate relationship, or the fact that we hadn't had sex, that they would find most shocking? What we have is companionship, commitment, care and affection. For my part, I can say they are qualities that are a lot more stable than what I found in most of the romantic relationships I've been in.

The Hamster and the Grumpy Goblin

Picture the scene, a lost and perplexed hamster wondering around a burning maze. Dramatic music plays in the background, lava bubbles underneath, as the little fur ball balances precariously on a rickety bridge made of lollipop sticks. There's no time for hesitation, however, as a horde of zombies is in hot pursuit of the little rodent. If the hamster makes it to the other side and avoids the large spinning discs covered in knives, it will then come face to face with an evil cat with razor-sharp teeth.

So, who would have thought that as a 54-year-old man I would become fascinated with hamster escape videos on YouTube? These are homemade cardboard box mazes where you follow a hamster navigating its way around pretend dangers in a bid for freedom. Milly has got me hooked and we love watching them together, both making predictions as to each hamster's strengths and weaknesses. Milly thinks grey hamsters are the bravest, but I am firm in my conviction that brown hamsters have the best problem-solving skills. If you are ever in our company, however, please, whatever you do, do not disrespect golden hamsters. We are united in our belief that they are numero uno of the hamster world. To state otherwise is to enter an argument you simply will not win.

As you might have guessed, this chapter is about Milly. This will of course be a biased daddy appraisal, but I wanted to give you a brief insight into her world. My daughter is a happy, confident, fun-loving and sociable young girl. She is infectious and enchanting in equal measure. She loves to learn, play and has a wonderful sense of humour.

On our daddy day outings, we love nothing better than to construct fantasy worlds we can lose ourselves in. Whether it's a trip into outer space or a visit to the pixie house we have built in our local woods, we get to act out our favourite characters to our heart's content.

We went to visit the pixie house just the other day only to find someone had knocked it down! We were stunned. Who could have committed such a heinous crime? In my ignorance, my first assumption was that it could have been local school kids. It turned out I couldn't have been more wrong. After a bit of a chin rub, Milly informed me it must have been the grumpy goblin who lives on the other side of the woods. 'Everybody' knows he is jealous of the pixie's house because he has to live in a damp bog that is full of stinging nettles and old crisp packets. I don't blame him really, but of course we had to do the right thing and give him a good telling off. As we approached the bog, I asked Milly if she would like to do that talking, but she informed me this was one of those particular tasks that fell under the specialist category of a 'daddy job.' So I found myself stood on the edge of a muddy bog calling out to a bad tempered Goblin that had a somewhat justified accommodation grievance. Unfortunately, this wasn't a skill set that hadn't been covered in the parenting guides I had read so far. I soon discovered that the trick is not to be put off by the dog walkers giving you funny looks. You are in too deep by this point, so just stick your guns. Getting the Goblin onside required some of my finest negotiation tactics and a Mars Bar. Which, if it enables the pixies to live in peace, I think you will agree, is a fair exchange.

When I told Mindy I was writing this book, she agreed to a quick interview in the car on the way to feed the ducks in the local park. This is how it went.

'Daddy's writing a book.'

'Why?'

'As a record of you me and mummy.'

Milly smiled. 'Will I be famous?'

'Do you want to be?'

'No.'

'Then you won't be. I'd love for you to tell me about some of your favourite hobbies though.'

'Jumping on my trampoline, collecting teddy bears, learning about lots of things, especially dinosaurs. Doing stuff with mummy. Looking after my guinea pig and cuddling my pets. Horse riding and I love ice skating and go twice a week. Once with mummy and once with you daddy, I am good at lapping you.'

'That's true. Most of the time, I'm trying not to fall over. What's your favourite food?

'I love fish and chips. I love ham with vinegar on it. Pears, red apples and big green grapes. Oh, and Pretzels. I also like eating mummy and daddy's food.'

'You also like giving daddy's food to Bella (the dog) too, don't you?' (That got an enormous smile and a nod)

'What are your favourite games?'

'Hide and seek, follow the leader and Paw Patrol rescue missions. And that game where I throw Guinea Pig droppings at you daddy.'

'That's not daddy's favourite game.'

'Also, whatever games my besties are playing.'

'It's great you have some best friends.'

'Yeah, I love them.'

'What else do you do with them?'

'We go to horse care and look after the horses. I love doing that.'

'You play drums in a band too, don't you?'

'Yes, with my bestie Heidi.'

'What kind of band is it?

'We're called The Pop Stars and we have two drummers and we've written two songs.'

'I've seen you play; you are really good. Can daddy join your band as a singer?'

Mindy thought about it. 'No. But you can take photographs.'

'Daddy used to sing in band,' I explained, trying to highlight my credentials.

'It's never going to happen, daddy.'

'What are you going to do when you grow up?'

'I've been thinking about that. I'm going to be a zookeeper with my other bestie Leo. We're going to work on a farm with the animals and sell lemonade as well.'

'That's a good plan honey, and when you when you make lots of money, will you support your dear old dad?

'No, you can make your own money, daddy.'

(There go my retirement plans).

Milly wrapped up the interview with a question for me. 'Daddy, is it normal for a man of your age to watch Hamster Escape?'

I didn't answer as I'm pretty sure that was a rhetorical question.

Hey Rae!

So far, you have had the unbridled pleasure of me shooting my mouth off. You have also heard from the unparalleled wisdom of Milly. Now the time has come to hear Rae's perspective. This, of course, will just be an overview because of the space we have available. What I was interested in for this book is what lead Rae to decide to choose this path and what she would have changed about how we went about things. At the end of the book, I have also interviewed a friend of mine called Hannah about her alternative parenting decisions, which brings us another perspective. I hand you over to Rae.

How did you find out about platonic co-parenting?

A friend of mine saw an article in the Independent newspaper magazine and said, 'Oh, look at this.' I had recently split up with my partner and she knew I wanted kids. She handed me the article, and I took it away and thought about it. After not long at all, I decided, *yeah, that's the way to go.* And that's what I decided I was going to do.

Why did I choose to take this path?

Because of my age and my history of relationships. My relationships hadn't worked out and at 42, I didn't have enough time to seek a traditional set-up. It takes too long before you know they will work, and that's before you decide if you're going to have kids together. Co-parenting seemed much more simple to be honest because you don't have to navigate the relationship stuff. It's all just about having a child.

Did you have any preset notions of what you were looking for in a co-parent?

No, I think I was just jumping in, really. The only thing that I was sure I needed was similar parenting styles and a similar sense of morality. After that it was the practicalities of how far away someone lives. Is that going to work? Are they employed? Are they self-sufficient? That kind of stuff.

What can you remember about our early meetings and any feelings, thoughts that came up for you putting our co-parenting agreement together, for example?

I remember meeting up once a week, sometimes once a fortnight. And I thought it was all going very well. We were going through suggested agreements and stuff. And I was keen to crack on and see that everything that we were thinking was similar enough to make things workable. I wanted to get to a place where we could see we had enough similarities and thoughts of where we were going as co-parents. I remember we thought we'd be like divorced parents that weren't in dispute. With a co-parenting agreement that a lot of divorced parents already have in place.

Is there anything you feel we should have gone about differently in our planning?

Not in the planning. I remember the one difficulty I found was that our personalities were very different. I would have done more regular meeting up because sometimes we didn't, and in hindsight, I would have met up at different places and do different activities. As that fits more with my personality. I make friends more easily by going bowling, for instance, rather than meeting in a pub for a drink. You seem to make friends in most situations, whereas I make friends more easily, in certain situations, if that makes sense. So actually, not only was it looking at parenting stuff, we needed to look at our own individual personality traits, too. Which actually, is quite tricky to do, I think with someone that you don't know very well, because it kind of can leave you quite vulnerable. It would have been finding a way looking of doing that in a fun and safe way. It was fine once everything looked as if it was

going to work. It was the deeper level of the trust which you got to first,
I think.

Here and Now

This brings me to the present day. And the perfect place to answer this question. 'Having got as far as you have, would you now have done anything differently? Even though I found the co-parenting dynamic emotionally challenging for the first few years, I wouldn't change any of it for the world. Why? Because I have the most amazing daughter imaginable. When I look at Milly. I realise it is platonic co-parenting that brought her to me and for that, I will be eternally grateful. Co-parenting is still a learning curve. A practice in self- improvement, patience and understanding, but then isn't any relationship, job or situation in life? Especially if we want to do it well?

A certain number of challenges are a useful growth opportunity if approached wisely. It is in these situations that you can develop the relationship you want with your co-parent. I have got things wrong at times, but I have tried to stay open to feedback from Rae. Being an engaged student of co-parenting is a mind-set I try to maintain. I want to keep an active intention to keep learning and growing in my role. The secret to our success so far is that Rae and I have been able to navigate our challenges. Because Rae and I have a mutual respect and a shared purpose, Milly will hopefully be able to witness and learn from the emotional maturity between us. I hope she will form relationships based on these values. Rather than spending time on the inevitable stress that often arises in romantic partnerships, Rae and I can focus on educating and having fun with Mindy. She is also far less likely to be in the middle of parental disputes and arguments. In fact, this hasn't happened once in 8 years.

The motivation for this book started out as a rather brief document describing my thoughts and aspirations behind why I decided to co-parent without romance. I also wanted to express my immense gratitude to Rae and Milly. I would like to say a massive thank you to Rae. Her capacity for fairness, patience, and good communication is awe-inspiring. Her emotional intelligence is unparalleled in my experience. She is one of the most empathic principled and humble people I've ever met. The level of dedication and care she has shown as a mother is incredible. I feel very lucky to be on this journey with her. I am excited by our journey, watching our daughter grow and seeing what the future brings. Should you choose this path, I wish you the same luck with your co-parent.

Platonic co-parenting is working for us, but I'm not saying it would work for everyone. Like with any relationship, it takes work. I believe you have to be interested and engaged. You need compassion, to be ready to learn and up for a challenge. You will then reap the rewards. There has been an increasing amount of interest in co-parenting in recent years. I asked Ivan Fatovic, Founder & CEO of Modamily what his views on theuturee of this family structure are.

'Our traffic and revenue tripled in 2021, where people just got more interested, I think we were in the Guardian around that time. I don't know if (co-parenting) is going to supplant the traditional way people do things, but it's definitely going to grow. I think the younger generation identify in so many different ways. Maybe they're non-binary. Maybe they don't see themselves being with one person for the rest of their lives. So, they are exploring other options. I think there's a lot of new relationships dynamics being formed and that's only going to grow.[17]

What I am proposing is that this family option should be an acceptable addition to the menu of family choices. As people's relationship needs morph and grow in line with the ever-changing personal and political events of life, our menu of family options needs to be as equally diverse and inclusive. Platonic co-parenting is an effective, caring, and creative solution to our changing times.

Plea From the Author

You made it to the end! I hope you enjoyed it. I would like to thank you for the opportunity to share my story with you. If you enjoyed the book, it would be amazing if you could leave a review for me. The amount of positive reviews the book has effects how visible it is in the online book swamp. This also helps me to continue with my writing adventure. Thanks in advance, it means the world.

Zoom Chats

Both Rae and I offer Zoom chats to anyone who would like to talk further about platonic co-parenting. We aren't authorities on the subject just people who have chosen this lifestyle and are living the co-parenting path. You can make contact via my website: www.nickfarrow.work[1]

For press and media inquiries you can also reach me via my website.

---

1. http://www.nickfarrow.work

The Winding Path of Life

It's not just me that takes on these harebrained schemes. A good friend of mine called Hannah was happy to share her journey for an alternative family, similar to the process that I've taken. I was particularly interested in capturing Hannah's thinking process. Why would an attractive heterosexual woman with no shortage of male suitors choose to go this route? I kicked off our interview with this question:

Hi Hannah, when did you first start thinking about Platonic co-parenting as a realistic option?

I always assumed I'd be a mother. I always wanted to have a family and for the last ten years I've been actively trying to make this happen. I had what I call my plan A route, which was meeting someone organically and having a family together. But for one reason or another, I just went through relationship after relationship, sometimes breaking up before even getting to the family planning stage. Most women have a biological clock ticking, which gets louder and louder the older you get. There was a point when, after a few years of being single – I was probably reaching my late 30s – I thought *Oh my God, what happens if I don't meet someone to have a family with? What am I going to do?* Until you introduced me to the idea of Platonic co-parenting, I don't think I'd ever heard of it before. It was when I got back from a trip to India and I guess the more I thought about it and the deeper I delved into it, the more I realised what a good solution it could be. It opened me up to this whole new world of possibility and suddenly I had a plan B.

How did you go about starting off and finding potential co-parents when you'd actually come to the decision that you wanted to explore this possibility?

I began with thinking of men I already knew who might have been interested in the idea. I also joined about three co-parenting websites. This was interesting because I was actually dating at this point as well, and co-parenting/sperm donor websites are very similar to dating websites. The profile that you put on each one is obviously very different, however!

It's hard to know when you're on a dating site if you're going to scare everyone off, if you're honest and say you're looking for someone to have children with. That's really hard in my experience as a woman, as it's not very common to find men who also really want to have children. Or at least who admit that from the beginning. When I met people through the co-parenting site, we'd get into the nitty-gritty straight away. As we both wanted to have children, which is obviously a massive deal, we needed to figure out if we were compatible enough to do that together.

Did you have a sense of what criteria you were looking for in a person?

I did have some very specific criteria: he had to be a non-smoker and we needed to have shared values; I didn't want any opposing religious or political views. But it was more about the feeling I had for them. You're trying to work out if they'll make a good father, but also whether we can become good friends. In a way, you're interviewing someone to be a close friend, which is quite an unusual thing to do.

There were two main contenders who I met several times each, and they were incredibly different from each other. I found it really hard to tell if they were suitable, because I was trying to get to know them quite deeply, quite quickly, which is a hard thing to do. You have to launch in with the really big questions straight away to find out how someone wants to raise their children. Which can only be a good thing really, as this isn't something people usually stop to think about. They often just get pregnant, have the child and then figure it out from there!

What experiences did you have when you met up with the prospective co-parents?

The first guy I met a few times for coffee and walks along the seafront. After a few meetings I got the impression he would have been a good friend, but I wasn't convinced he'd make the right kind of father for me. I was realising there were so many aspects to take into consideration.

The second guy was older. We met up quite a few times, had lots of good conversations and it was looking quite hopeful. But then he seemed to pull back and said he wasn't sure because he might be moving to Canada. That was confusing. He eventually told me he had moved to Canada, but I'm sure I saw him walking through town six months later!

Around this time I also made contact with someone I've known since my early 20s who was interested in co-parenting. It was a bit of a unique situation because, when I raised the idea with him and went through it all and how it could work, he said his preferred way would be to have things as close to a traditional setup as possible. He actually wanted to live together and offered to buy us a house. So, the idea was that we'd become a family, living in the same house, but we'd be in a Platonic relationship. It sounded great at the time, as it offered security, family and friendship. There was already trust and respect there from having known each other for so many years.

So we began the process. We started looking for a house to buy and began trying to get pregnant. Little did I know at the time that many of my friends and family had concerns about whether this was the right situation for me. But then a spanner in the works came along anyway when I met somebody in a dating situation. At the beginning I thought I could handle having a romantic relationship with one person whilst entering a co-parenting relationship with another. However, I soon realised that was asking for trouble. It was obviously a very difficult situation and I felt incredibly guilty for putting a stop to it, but in hindsight I think it was probably the best thing for both of us. I'm not sure it would have worked out the way either of us had hoped.

So then I found myself back in a plan A situation for a couple of years. We were trying for a baby for about a year, but then unfortunately we broke up. After this, I started grieving and letting go of the idea of being a mother at all, as I was now 45 by this point. However, as time passed, and fuelled by a close friend having a near-death experience, I realised I wasn't ready to fully let go of being a mother. So, I'm now open to trying all approaches, including plan C – sperm donors – and we'll see what happens.

Thanks for talking with me, Hannah.

Co-Parenting Agreement Issues

This information has been supplied for you courtesy of the: Baby Legal Law Firm

www.BabyLegal.net

The following is a list of topics and potential issues to be included in your co-parenting agreement. A co-parent agreement is about the division of rights and responsibilities between parents and ensuring that each has a say in their child's upbringing. Also, it is about personal preferences and should be tailored to each parent's expectations and desires. Some of these issues will not fit your circumstance or will not be important to you, whereas there may be some additional issues that you would like to include.

1. Residency and custody

a. Percentage of time resident with each parent

i. Residential scheduling

ii. Visitation plans

iii. Division of holidays b. Sole or joint legal custody c. Child's legal last name

2. Decision making

a. IVF/fertility i. Genetic testing of parents and/or embryos b. Pregnancy i. If advised to terminate a pregnancy for medical reasons, who decides? c. Childhood i. Spontaneous or emergency decision-making guidelines d. Emergency procedures i. Long-term legal procedures during emergencies ii. Alternative guardians

3. Financial Responsibility

a. Division of child support b. Duration of child support i. Through college? c. Tax issues i. You are advised to seek advice from a tax attorney/accountant ii. Both parents cannot claim the child as a dependent, so may choose to alternate years

4. Death a. Estate planning

i. This should be in place by the 2nd trimester of pregnancy b. Life insurance i. 20yrs term life is recommended Page 2 of 2 Baby Legal Law Firm // Co-Parenting Agreement Issue List

5. Third parties a.

Dating

i. Introducing dates to the child

b. Relationships

i. Introducing partners to the child

c. Grandparents

i. Grandparent visitation plans

6. Parenting Issues

a. Parental roles and responsibilities

b. Childcare

c. Discipline i. Bedtimes by age

d. Morals and family values

e. Gift-giving guidelines

f. Diet and nutrition

g. Medical care

h. Internet usage and TV/video game time

i. Social media usage

j. Transportation (between parents and otherwise)

k. Dating rules for child

7. Long-term parental expectations

a. Education i. Educational requirements

b. College

c. Extra-curricular activities d. Sports

8. Communication

a. How often will parents communicate re: child b. How will absent parent communicate with child

9. Religion

a. Will child be raised in a faith? b. Religious education

10. Confidentiality

a. If and when the parties may reveal details of their arrangement b. Naming the parties via private forum, public forum, social media

Nick and Rae's Co-Parenting Agreement

Our life philosophy and values

All decisions made should centre around and be in the best interests of the child.

The child will grow up in a liberal minded environment of love and acceptance.

Any disagreements between any of the parents to be kept away from the child.

For the parents to not speak ill of each other in front of the child

To never use of manipulate the child in any way as a result of any disagreement.

Consistency in child-rearing practices, we agree to keep regular contact with each other about our ongoing parenting practice.

Don't make assumptions

Be true to yourself

Be impeccable with your word

Try to judge as little as possible

Continued growth and self-awareness

Live to eat, not eat to live

Trust yourself and you will know how to live

Acceptance of others and self-acceptance

Patience

Nature of our friendship

We would like our friendship to continue to develop and strengthen, and for this to be the platform for our parenting skills to build on. We aim to share our own

emotional or other needs for support should we need to.

Decision-making

All big decisions and we consult each other; small decisions and we trust each other. We always keep each other informed when we feel it's a significant or the other parent would be interested. We always put the child at the heart of our decisions.

Parental Responsibility

Both Rae and Nick will be on the birth certificate and as such both will have

parental responsibility for the child/children.

Contact

It is Nick's intention to have regular and consistent contact

Rae is happy for Nick to have as much contact is as feasible.

Weekly contact (minimum once a week) by Nick

Contact by Nick's parents every 2-3 weeks

We will organise regular contact revolving around Nick and Rae's work commitments, the child's needs and our needs

Contact length and type will increase and change as the child grows up

Being flexible when needed, as long as it doesn't affect the security of the child

We will also build in time for discussions/decision making etc away from the child contact time, and away from the child. This will continue irrespective of new partners - but being aware that long-term partners may need to be included at some stage. Our sense is that this would be after 18months.

Christmas we would like to spend together whenever possible (even part of the day) however if this is not possible to alternate Christmas and Boxing Day each year.

During the period that the children are in the care of the alternate parent, no restrictions will be made on either Nick or Rae in seeing the children.

Birthdays - the children's birthdays will be shared by Rae and Nick regardless of which parent has responsibility on that particular day. Responsibility for arranging birthday parties will be shared by both Nick and Rae.

Respecting boundaries. When the child is with one parent, it is inappropriate for the other parent to make demands that will affect the quality of time the parent has with the child.

Nick and Rae would like to be known as: Muma/Mum/Daddy/Dad.

New Partners

No new partners will have parental responsibility.

It is very important for any new partner to be on board with Nick and Rae's parenting values and to mirror our parenting style.

We would both minimize contact with the child has with the new partner until such time comes when either of us are in a lasting, long-term relationship. We feel this should be at least 18months.

The potential worries, concerns and feelings of threat around Rae's or Nick's new partner(s) would be good for us to be able to talk about in complete confidentially, to put our minds at rest.

Childcare

We both share a commitment to balanced parenting with self-awareness being key. It is vital to show and verbalize our love for our child as well as show tactile affection. It is also very important the child has clear boundaries to operate within.

Rae will not work for the first year - she will take the full maternity leave.

Rae will go back to work part-time, with child tax credits

Nick and Rae will try to find creative ways around childcare, to include willing family support. Nick to create an online list system people can refer to and update.

The home of both Nick and Rae will each be furnished as a home for the child. Each parent will clean and take care of the clothes the children wear during their stay with each parent. The children will bring or leave any small toys at either home at their discretion although the parents should undertake to return the items as soon as is convenient. This should not be the responsibility of the children.

Nick and Rae will be flexible. If there is something that benefits our child that does not negatively impact your timesharing (or you are willing to make an exception), try to accommodate the other parent.

We will consider our child's needs first and foremost, and try to strike a balance between the "needs" and the "wants." Most children need structure in their daily lives, but they also need some down-time. Filling every afternoon with an activity may seem fun and create a well-rounded child, but studies have also shown that an overly busy schedule may also create unnecessary stress on a child. Remember also that children typically want to please both of their parents, and what is said to one parent may differ vastly from what is said to the other parent. That's why it is important for Nick and Rae to have regular updates with each other.

Acceptance of Different Styles within reason. It would be unusual for two parents to have exactly the same parenting styles. People have legitimate differences around issues of bedtimes, food, TV, discipline and risk tolerance. Cooperative parenting requires that each parent resist the temptation to criticize the other parent's parenting unless there is a serious danger to the child. The cost of the criticism and the predictable defence and counter criticism usually exceeds by far whatever benefits are sought in the first place. Children need their parents to be at peace so biting one's tongue may be a vitally important behavior. When this is not possible, choose an appropriate time and place to talk. With this regard both Nick and Rae agree to introduce and practice the **"Rule of three"** This is for smaller issues that we are finding it hard to let go of. On the first time we notice the issue we vow not to say anything but to act after it has happened three times. The second time it happens we notice how it feels. Is it still an issue? If so, we vow to speak about it calmly after the third time it happens. For both Nick and Rae to foster a culture of open communication where we feel able to communicate our needs to each other.

When the child asks either of us why we are not together, we will have decided in advance as to what to say.

In the event of illness or death or extreme emotional breakdown and the primary care giver is unable to parent effectively then the other parent would become the primary care giver. If he became unable, then Nick's Mother and Rae's brother would take over as the child's guardians. This would be reviewed yearly as at some point it may include long-term partners. Whoever the child's primary care giver is, regular access to extended family is very important.

All big decisions about the child including medical and dental treatments, (except in extreme emergency) will be made between Nick and Rae. Each parent reserves the right to attend medical appointments with the children regardless of who is responsible for them on that day.

<u>Finance</u>

Nick will use the Child Support Agency guidelines/calculator found here (https://www.gov.uk/calculate-your-child-maintenance) to pay a regular child maintenance on time via direct debit.

If Rae is having trouble affording any big items to speak to Nick to see if he can afford to contribute and/or seek family assistance when needed. Nick to set up an online list that family members can access and amend if they are able to source anything on it.

Cot mattresses and car seats to be new, most other things can be sourced cheaply/secondhand. Nick to also support Rae with sourcing free items on freecycle.

We agree to both take out wills. In Nick's will he would secure Rae's ongoing maintenance costs until the child/children is 18 and then leave money for the child to use for a specific purpose to help get established in life. i.e., to put towards an education or mortgage. In Rae's will, she will do the same for Nick, as he would them become the child's primary care giver.

We agree to set up a child trust fund and start to save as much money as we can for the child to access when the child is 18 for education needs or 21 for a deposit towards a mortgage.

Religion

Conventional religion is not important to either of us; spiritual values are. Values such as kindness, generosity, acceptance of self and others, happiness at others success, humility, compassion, cooperation and truthfulness. These values and the over all spiritual growth of the child to be nurtured. It is important to give the child the choice to make up their own mind.

Education

Look for the best available school in the area. Look into available bursaries/scholarships.

Naming on the birth certificate

Both Nick and Rae to be named on the birth certificate.

Naming the child

The child's surname will be double-barrelled

First/Second name a work in progress

Multiple births

We are open to discussing one more child after the first child/children.

Location

Given our awareness of the article synopsis below we will try to plan towards living closer to each other as possible. Both of us want to stay in Sussex and aim to move closer together when and if this becomes possible.

Our role in each other's extended family

For both Nick and Rae to have as close ties as possible with each others families.

Conflict Resolution

Stage 1) Sort it ourselves through dialogue.

Stage 2) Ask an impartial friend to mediate if we are struggling to sort it ourselves

Stage 3) Professional mediation to be organized if both of the above is not successful.

Acknowledgments

In no particular order. I owe massive thanks to all of the following beings:

Milly: because she's amazing.

Rae: because she is cool.

Tracy, Samson, Martina, Liz, Wook, Tamzin, Andy, Peter, for very valuable feedback and insight.

S.T. for content editing, proof reading, photos, video, moral filter and brother.

Bobby J: Ideas and sounding board guru. My comedy muse in human form.

Claude for ongoing moral support.

Ma and Pa: For support, feedback and encouraging me all the way.

Karen Bonnell for input, insight and support.

Ivan from Modamily for support and networking

Judith Stacey for insight.

Emma Willing for legal insight.

Thomas S. Gleeson, Esq. for legal insight.

Dr. Lauren Brim for input and insight.

Thomas for therapeutic insight.

Laurence B for therapeutic insight.

Karen and Ruth for helping me believe it was possible.

And all my lovely friends for listening to me.

Copyright

Diary of a Platonic Co-Parent
COPYRIGHT 2023 © Nick Farrow
All Rights Reserved.
First edition.

---

[1] canterburylawgroup.com/divorce-statistics-rates

[2]   https://www.marriage.com/advice/divorce/surprising-divorce-facts-and-statistics

[3]   https://www.ons.gov.uk/peoplepopulationandcommunity/birthsdeathsandmarriages/divorce

[4] You can find out more about Dr. Lauren Brim on her website at www.laurenbrim.com

[5] Thomas S. Gleeson, Esq. Attorney at Law at Baby Legal. www.babylegal.net

[6] Emma Willing, Partner (Family Team) www.mishcon.com

[7] https://www.researchgate.net/profile/Elizabeth-Gould-4

[8] Thomas Larkin is an integrative psychotherapist/counsellor, supervisor and trainer with a practice in Dublin city. You can find him online here: https://thomaslarkin.ie

[9]   https://hekint.org/2020/03/20/michel-de-montaigne-in-his-circular-library

[10]   https://www.theguardian.com/world/2021/dec/03/recorded-homophobic-hate-crimes-soared-in-pandemic-figures-show

[11]   https://prismreports.org/2022/04/20/hate-crimes-rise-anti-lgbtq-legislation

[12] The New England Journal of Medicine www.nejm.org[1]

[13] Medical Journal of Australia - www.mja.com.au[2]

[14] https://en.wikipedia.org/wiki/Back_to_Basics_(campaign)#Scandals https://www.independent.co.uk/news/two-months-of-sex-and-sleaze-1392667.html

[15] You can discover more about Karen on her website: www.KarenSBonnell.com

[16] https://www.americanprogress.org

[17] You can discover more about Ivan and Modamily at his website www.modamily.com

---

1. http://www.nejm.org/

2. http://www.mja.com.au